A postcard from East Africa

A survival guide

Rupnarayan Bose

A postcard from East Africa

ISBN: 9798894465821

Publisher: Notion Press, Chennai, India

Cover design: Siddhartha Bose

Disclaimer:

The content of this book is solely for the purpose of light reading. Readers should obtain the latest information from appropriate sources before taking any action including travel. This author, the publishers or the references/sources quoted in this book take no responsibility whatsoever for the consequences arising out of any action taken or not taken by any person based on its contents.

CHAPTER INDEX

AUTHOR'S NOTES

It's a postcard that was written two decades back but arrived only now.

This book took shape in response to the large number of queries about Africa put to me by people who telephoned or dropped in at very short notice, immediately after I returned from East Africa in 2001. Some were curious about visiting Africa as a tourist; wanted a travel plan. Others wanted to know about what terms to negotiate for with his/her future employer, the pros and cons of taking up assignments in Africa, the quality of life and so on.

Some had heard about the risks, and so wanted the 'real' story. All of them calling on me had the same objective – to obtain first-hand information regarding the place they were thinking of visiting. None of them had been to Africa before, some had information that was vague, so felt the need to know 'at least something concrete' about the place before embarking on a trip.

Simple, elementary or basic queries led to lengthy discussions. Having faced these questions from time to time, I thought it better to record all these issues, and some of the information that I had the occasion to pass on during these encounters, so that others similarly interested may benefit from it (and I don't have to repeat myself ad infinitum)

This book is the outcome of my few years' experience in East Africa. It reflects the learning process that I myself went through years ago as a first-time visitor to Africa. I have to clarify that my experience was limited only to the East African countries. It would, therefore, be a grave error to paint all the countries with the same brush. For the first-time visitor to Africa, the tips given in the following pages should act only as a beginner's guide, a starting point, nothing more.

I have outlined what a new visitor should be aware of while considering taking up a job in Africa, and what he or she may expect. In essence, the probable risk factors – both in their personal and in their professional lives. The reason is that in sharp contrast to a person visiting Africa (or any foreign country for that matter) as a mere tourist or as a short-term visitor, a person relocating with a new assignment in a new country must make commitments of a more serious nature. He must take a few hard decisions that a casual visitor (for example) may not be required to take. These commitments, these decisions have far greater implication for the person concerned, or her family for quite some time to come.

After reading this book he may be in a better position to ask the right questions, get his doubts cleared, know how to deal with the probable minefields and (hopefully) take a better-informed decision with regard to his future. (For example, I made a big mistake by asking my family to shift along with me to Africa. On hindsight, the risks and the price that I had to pay would have been far less if I had gone there without my family members in tow. But who was there to tell me about these options, the pros and the cons? Hopefully, anyone reading this book may not have to experience what I had to.)

For those planning their first ever trip to the African continent this book could be a useful guide. (Even as late as in March 2024 my friends planning to visit the Mara or Ngorongoro are asking me for details about Africa.) Make sure that you obtain the latest information from appropriate authorities when you plan for any trip.

Many people from other parts of the world (including India) have stayed back in the African countries that they were (presumably) visiting for a short period, adopted those countries as their homes, and eventually acquired their citizenship. Many are living there quite happily, benefiting from all that the various countries in Africa have to offer.

On my part, I must say that I have immensely enjoyed my stay in East Africa. The gains have far outweighed the so-called risks. I had loads of fun, was about to be shot dead, saw places of unsurpassed beauty rarely to be seen in any other part of the world, met a large number of very gentle, courteous and friendly people – of Kenyan, Ugandan and other nationalities. Many of them are still my very good friends. I am richer by my experience, and thankful for the opportunity to have lived in Africa. I would be happy to go back there – any day.

The information and comments contained in the chapters that follow are furnished with the best of intentions. However, the author or the publisher of this book assume no responsibility for any observation and consequence arising out of any change in position or any action taken by any reader of this book as a result of any comment or suggestion contained herein.

The views and perceptions expressed in this book are exclusively this author's own. No bias or offence of any kind is intended to any country, place, people, race, religion or culture of any denomination.

I went back to Nairobi, Kenya in 2003, but that was my last visit to this beautiful country. This book was written around that period immediately after my final return from Africa.

Two decades have passed since then. In order to retain the original flavour, I have not updated the information in this book. The ground realities could be different as on date (for example, the visa rules for visit to Kenya has been relaxed considerably lately). Hence, caveat emptor. Take the contents of this book as nothing more than a fun-read, a blast from the past, and savour the contents.

Enjoy the many wonders of Africa. It's as close to Mother Nature as one could get to be.

Have fun.

Rupnarayan Bose

01 March, 2005

(Slightly re-touched: June 2024)

CHAPTER I

IT IS NOT A COUNTRY, BUT A CONTINENT

(*and a very large one at that!*)

Everything said and done, going to a new country is a leap of faith – especially if one is going there for a longish stay. The move is likely to affect an individual's personal and professional life in a significant way. There are decisions to be taken. Preparations are to be made. Personal life has to be rearranged.

However much one may research one's destination, one cannot ignore the fact that the move will always be a leap in the dark. At best, one can make an attempt to identify the issues involved while seeking that patch of green, trying to reduce the uncertainties to the extent possible.

In the chapters that follow, I have tried to apprise the future traveller to Africa with as many points of relevance that I thought he or she should be aware of.

Going to Africa is not like travelling to USA or the UK. Our general knowledge about the developed countries is more (or, so we'd like to believe!) than our knowledge about the places like the countries in Africa, Central or South America. The yardsticks that we unconsciously tend to apply when we talk about the developed countries cannot be applied, simply by extrapolation, to the many countries that make up the continent of Africa. Every country is different, has its own characteristics and charm.

The reason for the variety is simply this: While discussing Africa, a point to keep in mind is that Africa is not *a single* country. It is made up of a combination of nations – fifty-four in all, of many hues and cultures. Except Ethiopia and Liberia, all the other countries had been under the influence of diverse occupying forces of varied nationalities. In consequence, they have acquired, and to some extent have adopted – for better or for worse – cultures of the nations that had ruled over them till their independence. Each country has its own system of governance, its own culture, its own preferences and priorities. The economy of each of these countries that add up to form the continent of Africa differ greatly from one country to another.

For example, right hand drive or left hand drive? Just ask your former colonial masters! They set the rules.

Malawi and Botswana are within the same continent of Africa, but are like chalk and cheese. The former is said to be the poorest country in the world. In contrast, Botswana is one of the most peaceful, economically a haven, and in natural beauty – incomparable.

Accordingly, the job situations also differ from country to country within the same land mass that is Africa. Unlike India, or Japan, or the U.S.A., or Canada a uniform approach or a general standard cannot be applied across the board to 'Africa'. *It is just not a single country*.

As has been said before, even grey has many shades. It is extremely difficult to do specific and individual justice to each. Nor is it possible (or practically advisable) to put in black and white issues that better be discussed only face to face for proper and fuller understanding of the many shades that make up the enchanting continent of Africa.

Therefore, the statements that follow are mostly general observations, and should only be considered as such.

CHAPTER II

DESTINATION EAST AFRICA

Westward Ho!

[Why westward? Because I had moved there from India. Why East Africa? Because this book is based mostly on my experience in East Africa. Beside the point, though.]

A survey (January 2004) conducted by the web edition of the Economic Times revealed that 45% of the sample responded with 'yes' to the question, "Are you planning to look for a job abroad this year?" Although 53% said 'no', 69% agreed that India Inc.

cannot ever match salaries paid abroad, while 28% were positive that India could, someday.[1]

When asked: "What do you look for in a foreign job?" of the respondents 57% said it was 'money', 28% indicated 'country' and 15% selected 'job profile'.

HR professionals, however, point out that the West is not as attractive as it once used to be. The salary differentials are narrowing. The sudden job losses (especially in the dream destination, USA) have been mounting. Simultaneously, there is far more opportunity in India today than was available a few years ago. The quality of life has caught up in many ways with the West. "It is even better" – say some. Yet, the above poll shows that the average Indian still has aspirations of going 'abroad'. Do note that 'abroad' in common parlance means one of the developed countries – especially the U.S., Canada and the UK – places where English is a medium of communication.

The yearning continues in spite of the ever-increasing entry restrictions being imposed by

---

[1] Well, in 2024, one can say that India *has* changed a lot, and radically so, since then.

(especially) the U.S. The debate in the U.S. over the L-1 visa (and the loopholes that are sought to be plugged) may not make things any easier in future.[2]

Alarm bells

"There is also a growing realization that the first-generation Indians in the U.S. and the U.K. are essentially second-class citizens. In the universities it may be a different picture. But in industry and society, immigrants are invariably discriminated against. Take salaries. An U.S. General Account's Office survey shows that U.S. employers get away with paying H1-B visa holders much less than what they should – 33% less by some estimates. Older workers, with less bargaining power, are victimized further." (The Telegraph Jobs, 10-Feb-2004)

An Economic Times report (11-February-2004) titled 'L-1 Bill back in focus after U.S. House hearing' has this to say: 'Sona Shah, whose testimony shed light on the world of the L-1, was former programmer analyst at Wilco Systems. Ms Shah testified (to the Sub-committee on International Relations of the

---

[2] In 2021 things are much different, with no small thanks to Covid-19, but this piece was written in 2004.

House of Representatives) to the fact that Indian recruits were severely underpaid.....'. The rush for BPO and body shopping only confirms this view.

Some facts of life!

Extracts from two letters published in The Telegraph, Calcutta on 11-November-2003 – in response to a report on Canada as a favourite destination – had this to say:

Extracts from the first letter-

"Most Indians who consider Canada an extension of the United States of America are miserable in the end. Canada, in fact, is ill-suited to Indians who, much like the Americans, live in a dog-eat-dog world where powerful members of the society thrive at the cost of their less fortunate compatriots. The people of Canada have drawn important lessons from past iniquities regarding social justice, equality and the sharing of resources. Canada expects its citizens to struggle and share. So Canada should not be seen as substitute destination for people who wish to go to the US or Britain. There are far too many Indians here who despise the weather, the lack of

aggression and the lack of creature comforts."
(Shyamal Bagchee, Edmonton, Canada)

Extracts from the second letter-

"I feel a strong urge to warn potential applicants to Canada every time I hear about immigration lawyers selling the Canadian dream. For one, the dream can work only after years and years of struggle. Having immigrated to Canada seven years back, I realize that very little about us is actually recognized here – be it education, work experience or driving skills. On an average, newcomers have to wait for four to six months to find work at the clerical level. Poverty among the new immigrants is high and the conditions are far worse now than they were 10 years ago. For new immigrants it means starting from scratch. I have seen chartered accountants working as accounts clerks, qualified doctors as security guards and engineers from premier Indian Institutions as parking lot attendants or call centre staff. Local employers do not recruit new immigrants for their lack of 'experience'. There is actually a vast gap between what the Canadian government projects and the ground realities." (Debu Banerjee, Ontario, Canada)

Fast forward to December 2022

Karla Briones, Immigrant Serial Entrepreneur, Business Strategist for Underrepresented Entrepreneurs Small Business Columnist, TEDx Speaker and Business College Lecturer has this to say (posted on Linkedin on 9-Dec-2022)

> My older brother is a foreign trained doctor. My dad is a foreign trained veterinarian. My mother is a foreign trained educator.
>
> My brother's first job: hospital orderly (literally he was only allowed to change hospital beds). My dad's first job: selling gas contracts from door to door. My mom's first job: cleaning homes.
>
> My brother never recertified (sic) and now works as a stress test technician in the Heart Institute. My dad recertified (sic) and eventually went to open his veterinary practice. He beat the odds. My mom left the education field all together.
>
> *We can do better Canada. We can do so much better.*

Jessica Wong (CBC News) in a post on 01 December 2022 quoted StatsCan saying that,

"…Many immigrants struggle to find placements in their chosen professions.…Canada not doing enough with its highly educated immigrants. ….Many face barriers getting back into chosen professions, researcher says".[3]

The grass on the other side…

Feedback received first-hand reveals that out of ten people who land up in Canada for permanent residence, six come back extremely disappointed, frustrated, and after losing all their savings that they had taken with them on migration. (You can easily meet them at the airports on your way to Canada). Of the remaining four, two hang on for dear life driven by their own compulsions. They live on pittance doing menial jobs, or with jobs far below their training or calling, but refuse to return. The remaining two make it to a decent living standard and life style after about three or four years of struggle and very hard work. What we, and the world

---

[3] https://www-cbc-ca.cdn.ampproject.org/c/s/www.cbc.ca/amp/1.6666984

at large, happen to see and are tempted by, are these last 'two' (the success stories) of the ten that migrate. The stories of the other 'eight' rarely, if at all, draw our attention.

Any country in the world, including those in the developed world, is sensitive about immigrants and its immigration laws. African countries are no exception – for reasons that are obvious and quite understandable. Any person taking up employment in a foreign land, on the basis of a 'work permit' or a 'working visa', would always be in a vulnerable position and subject to possible exploitation. It is a risk that is inherent in the arrangement (being a non-citizen). Selecting an employer of choice is, therefore, critical (more about this in a later chapter).

Irrespective of evidence to the contrary, optical illusion or not, not caring about who waters the grass on *this* side or *that*, the grass on the 'other side' (read 'abroad') will always appear greener than that nearer home. The craving to go abroad, to earn more, to enjoy a (supposedly) better quality of life and work environment, provide better opportunities to the children, would continue to be the main motivators for those seeking to migrate for greener pastures.

Looking beyond the highly developed countries

What I find interesting is that, while seeking a career abroad, or a country to emigrate to, the usual approach is to look westwards. Comfort with the English language makes Australia, New Zealand etc. and the south-east Asian countries among the other destinations of choice. It is still curious to note that very few consciously consider the countries in Eastern Europe, Russia, Africa or a South America as a 'preferred destination' – for a job, a career, or places to emigrate to. One would rather face all the hardships in the West than explore the relatively greater comforts and rewards that (say) Africa can offer (a case of the known devil being preferred over one not so well-known, may be!). If that be so, one can hardly be blamed. The reasons, and reservations, could be well appreciated.

But my experience in the few countries in Africa that I was fortunate to live in, tells me that the benefits from living in some of the African countries could be much more than the so-called drawbacks, the 'pluses' being more than the 'minuses', the quality of life could be amazing.

Every country has its share of dubious and illegal immigrants, and immigration laws (by whatever term defined) trying to control their countries' borders and the inflow. Countries in Africa are no exception. However, unlike the West European nations, there is neither a mad rush to emigrate to these countries by means fair or foul, nor is there a desperate attempt by those countries to raise every possible barrier and make it as difficult as possible for people from succeeding in that attempt. So, things are *relatively* easier. Several of these countries, on the other hand, welcome qualified professionals who can add value to the overall output.

Yes, a citizen of any country would enjoy certain rights and advantages over one who is *not* one. But, if he minds his own business, an expatriate can enjoy life to the fullest from the time he lands in Africa. As I said, the quality of life is far, far better than one can ever imagine or enjoy elsewhere.

Last, but not the least – if you love to travel, if you wish to observe first-hand the wonders of Mother Nature in all her raw and unspoilt beauty, there is no place on earth that you should be but in Africa (remember that most of the wild life you see on

National Geographic or Discovery Channels were shot in Africa!). And I have not yet talked about the leisurely and relaxed life style ('No hurry, no worry. This is Africa.' – they say), the simple joys of life ('Hakuna Matata – don't worry, be happy'), fabulous weekends, significantly higher pay package for expatriates, or the respect that you get for your knowledge and expertise as a professional.

Reasons enough to change your mind, your travel plans, and pull out the Atlas to select your destination? I can assure you that you'll have no reason to regret your decision.

Enjoy Africa. Observe Nature from close at her wondrous best. It will be a huge bonus.

CHAPTER III

THE WORKING VISA

Getting in

A 'visa' allows you to enter and stay in a country of which you are not a citizen, or don't hold that country's passport. Most of the African nations encourage tourism. A large percentage of their revenues accrue from the tourist traffic. Generally speaking, the easiest visa to obtain is the tourist visa. The period of stay under such visas could range from one to three months depending on the immigration rules of the country concerned and the purpose of your visit to that country.

'Visa-on-arrival'

In order to encourage tourism some countries had provided the facility to issue 'visa on arrival'. This meant that you did not have to apply for and obtain a visa *before* leaving your home country. On arrival, at the entry point – be it by land, sea or by air – you were issued a visa after filling up an application form and on payment of a small fee (say about US$50.00 to US$100.00). The visa was marked, pasted or stamped on your passport.

With the development of technology, eVisa has gained ground with the simultaneous discontinuation of visa-on-arrival.

Electronic Travel Authorisation (ETA)

Kenyan visas, called "electronic Travel Authorisation" (eTA), are now issued electronically. An eTA application, to be applied for before you travel, can easily be filed online and once approved, it would be electronically linked to your passport.

The eTA requirements, as specified by the Kenyan government, are an Indian passport with at least two blank pages, valid for at least six months from the date of arrival in Kenya, confirmation page of the application, a colour passport size photograph, current email address, a basic travel itinerary and the return ticket.

Obtain specific information

At the planning stage, it is advisable to check on the visa rules with respect to the country you intend to visit. The "visa on arrival" system is very convenient and trouble-free. It met the need of those times. Countries have mutual arrangements to extend certain immigration facility to each other's citizens. In several countries 'eVisa' has replaced visa-on-arrival. The fees are variable, depending on the country of origin of the visitor. So don't assume things. Verify the latest status before your journey.

A number of countries only allow single entry permits if the visitor applies for a 'visa on arrival'. If the visitor has any plans to go to neighbouring countries, and later return to the country first visited, he would normally need to possess a 'multiple entry' visa, not a 'single entry' visa. 'Multiple entry' visas may have to be obtained from the respective consulate or embassy of the country concerned located at the visitor's country of origin.

For example, South Africa would require that a citizen of India apply in advance to the South African consulate in India for a visa (either for single entry or multiple entry), and not 'on arrival' at the airport in Johannesburg. Further, under normal circumstances, an application for a visa to South Africa from a person on a temporary visit from India to (say) Kenya may not be processed by the South African Consulate or Embassy in Kenya. The Indian citizen's application would be forwarded to their office in India for processing. Alternately, he should go back to India and put in his application to the consulate or embassy concerned in his own country.

Hence, it is again advisable to check out these facts and the exact situation applicable to a specific country when planning a trip. If you are traveling on employment, your prospective employer will be able to provide the required information quite easily.

The 'work visa' or 'work permit'

Let us begin by addressing the issue of a document that will allow you to *work* in a foreign country. Rules and regulations that allow you to work vary from country to country. It depends on your status. It also depends on the immigration and relevant rules of the country concerned, and could be subject to change from time to time. The document that allows you to work in a foreign land is variously called a 'work permit', 'working visa', 'work visa' etc. Without this document, it is illegal if you take up any profession, or any employment, in a foreign country.

Caution:

Almost every government takes a very serious view of people seeking or soliciting employment while visiting a country as a tourist or in any other capacity. Hence, mixing business with pleasure should be strictly avoided. Violations could result in arrest (and jail) or immediate deportation.

The Kenyan HC, New Delhi, website says, "Engaging in any form of business or employment without a requisite permit or pass is an offence."

You have been warned.

The 'expat' – a necessary evil

Every country would like to give priority to its own people for jobs. An expatriate worker – or an immigrant – is therefore considered (sort of) a 'necessary evil'. An expatriate is permitted to come in where local expertise in an area is not available. But it is expected that, over time, that particular expertise and skill would be developed locally and the expat replaced with domestic work force.

The expatriate, thus, takes away a job that, in the normal course, a citizen should have been doing. The expatriate is perceived to own no allegiance to the country that gives him employment. On the contrary, he is sometimes seen as one who drains out the resources by sending his income out of that country, mostly to his own homeland. For these reasons, an expatriate worker is not loved or welcomed with open arms by many nations. They are tolerated at best, not necessarily loved or cherished in a foreign land. A person going overseas for a job needs to remember this fact of life at all times.

[I know that by stating the above, I am likely to invite criticism. The fact remains, there is a grain of truth in

the above. Hence these words of caution, coupled with the need to maintain a low profile and simply mind your own business while abroad. As I said earlier, what I am describing here is a general scenario. The influx of immigrants is an on-going issue in most of the developed countries around the world.]

The number of overseas workers is regulated at most places of work, and the employer is required to replace them with local people as early as possible. The immigration department normally keeps track of the actual number of expatriate staff employed with each organization, and seeks to put a cap on the proportion, and the number, that they would allow at each establishment, and within the country as a whole. In fact, an employer in Kenya is answerable to the Immigration Department if it has not been able to reduce the total number of expatriates employed over a period of time.

Yellow fever certificate

Take a yellow fever vaccination at least two weeks prior to your departure date. After you are vaccinated, you will be given a signed certificate. Laminate it, make copies, and carry the original with you for showing it at the immigration counters as and when asked to do so.

If you do not carry the certificate with you, you may be quarantined for a number of days before being permitted to enter a country (including India).

The employer as sponsor

The 'work permit' or 'work visa' is normally issued by the immigration department (or a department having similar responsibilities) of a country on application by the prospective employer acting as your 'sponsor'. It is for the employer, proposing to employ an expatriate, to justify the need of a foreigner to work in that position, and as to why a local person cannot serve the same purpose.

Facts you should know

The key points to be noted with regard to the role of the sponsor are as follows:

a) Without a job offer or an appointment letter from the sponsor in hand, you cannot even apply for an entry visa or working visa.

b) A significant amount is required to be paid by the sponsor as fee towards the application for a 'work permit'. (Try to ensure that it is not deducted from your future salary.)

c) The 'permit' is normally valid for a pre-defined period (say, of two or three years), and is subject to renewal on re-application by the sponsor. (Which means that you annoy them at your own cost!)

d) The renewal is at the sole discretion of the immigration authorities of the country concerned and its government, subject to rules and regulations in force at the time of processing a renewal application. Issue and factors – not necessarily those contained in the rule books – may influence decisions with regard to renewal applications.

e) In most cases, the employer-sponsor must stand surety to the good conduct of the expatriate.

f) Being the 'sponsor', the employer may, if he so chooses, apply at any time to the immigration department for withdrawal of its sponsorship and consequently the 'work permit'. If you cannot manage to obtain another sponsor and another 'work permit' before the earlier 'permit' expires, you would have no option but to pack your bags and leave that country.

g) The concerned government at any time may, at its own volition, and assigning no reason whatsoever, withdraw the permit to work or to stay within the country. You have practically no right to challenge that decision.

Work permit – Related issues

The implications are as follows:

a) One should not start work in *anticipation* of the 'work permit' being received; say immediately after the application has been submitted for the 'permit'. The possibility remains that the application for a 'working visa' could be rejected at any time and for no reason whatsoever. Hence, jumping the gun, reporting for duty in anticipation of the sanction of a 'work permit' and starting to work could be fraught with a huge amount of risk.

b) Therefore, one *should not* take up employment, or start one's work, till a proper 'work permit' has been issued by the concerned authorities, duly received by the employer and the expatriate, all formalities (for example, execution of a guarantee or an undertaking – as may be required by law – by the employer) have been completed, and all fees for the same have been paid. (Retain the original, or at least a photocopy, of the permit/visa with you at all times.) The risks of acting against the above is explained a little later in this chapter.

c) Generally speaking, some form of a credential, an ID document to prove your 'resident alien' (or by whatever name called) status, would be issued to you and your family members to establish your identity, and for inspection whenever necessary. It permits you to stay longer than a tourist or a person on a temporary business visit would be allowed to. Some countries issue a separate 'pass' authorizing your residency in that country.

In Kenya, for example, it is called an 'Alien Card'. It has your photograph, your address and signature on it. It must be renewed periodically, and serves as your identification. It should be produced whenever called for – especially to the inspecting agencies, like the immigration people or the police. If such a document is issued in the country where you live, please carry it with you at all times.

The 'Resident Alien' status also gives you certain benefits which a foreigner is not entitled to. So, have it around with you always. (Do not carry your passport on your person, since it is the most valuable document that you have, and can be misplaced or snatched from you at some point in time. Retain your passport in the safest – but a readily accessible – place, for reasons explained later.

d)   The employee is deemed a 'guest' of the country where he/she has taken up employment. One should do absolutely nothing that may upset the host, and must always respect the government of the country where one has taken up residence. The wisest course would be to mind one's own business, and enjoy the best that the country (and the continent) has to offer.

e)   The expatriate employee cannot take up, or switch to, another job within the same country without a 'no-objection' being issued by the employer who had originally 'sponsored' your visit and stay in that country. The new employer must again apply for a fresh 'permit' for employment, and can employ him only after all the formalities are duly completed.

f) Since the employee is in the country only at the will (pleasure) of his employer, he should ensure that the employer is kept in good humour at all times. The employee must ensure that the parting – whenever it comes – is always cordial. As the saying goes, "Do not bang the door shut; you may have to go back!"

In essence, you'd need a 'working visa' or a 'work permit' to enable you to stay and work in a foreign land. There are several approaches to it. The problems that you may have to encounter, and the probable risks involved are outlined below.

Incidental Risks and Options:

A) *Most prospective and responsible employers will ask you to wait till the 'working visa' is actually issued and is in hand before asking you to fly out of your own country.*

This is the best course of action, and such employers could be considered as the most decent and ethical in the treatment of their personnel. So, *wait* patiently till confirmation is received to the effect that a 'working visa' or a 'work permit' has indeed been issued in your favour. Request and obtain a copy by fax, e-mail, courier or WhatsApp *before* you leave on your trip. Carry a copy of the 'work permit' with you at all times when you leave your own country. The copy will be helpful at the emigration point of your country and at the entry point of the foreign country.

Inform your current employer about your decision to resign *only after* you have a copy of the 'work permit' in your hands. Since a 'work permit' or a 'working visa' could be denied or refused for many reasons, you could be caught out on a limb if you prematurely declare your intention to resign, and then find that the overseas job has disappeared for no fault of yours or of your sponsoring employer.

B)   *At times, the prospective employer may suggest that you to come over to the country concerned, with the assurance that the formalities would be completed in due course (meaning, after you have arrived in that country).*

This is the most dangerous of all situations, and should send alarm bells ringing. For reasons best known to yourself, if you happen to succumb to the offer or the suggestion, you may land in serious trouble: I say 'may', because the prospective employer could have made the request in good faith, and with the confidence and certainty that he *would* make the necessary arrangements in due course. And may be, he does, eventually.

Nothing wrong with that, nothing at all – provided everything goes well and according to plan. That is the 'up-side', and I'd be the first person to wish anyone 'good-luck' if things work out as planned and in one's favour.

The problem is with the 'down-side', **if** things do not go as promised or as planned. **If** things happen to go wrong somewhere down the line because of the employer or in spite of his best efforts. Then what?

Possible problem areas

Let me outline some of the pitfalls, dangers and problems in a worst-case-scenario that could visit 'an innocent abroad'. They are as follows:

i)   If the prospective employer has asked you to enter the country first, and promises to arrange a 'working visa' later, obviously he would have taken no step till then to apply for a 'working visa'. However, one can only assume that he could be completing the formalities and would have submitted the required application by the time you are in his country. (If not, does he plan to do so later? When?)

ii) In the absence of a 'working visa', your entry to the country concerned would *probably* be as a tourist, on a 'tourist visa'. As I have said earlier, such 'tourist visas' have a limited validity period, allow a visitor to stay within the country for a relatively short term, allowing you to enter the country only for a specific purpose – namely, tourism.

Such visas strictly *do not* allow a visitor to pursue any vocation or profession, take up a job, or allow a person to perform *any* task for remuneration or profit.

iii) Conclusion: Even if you enter the country of your prospective employer, *you are not permitted by law to work for him*. In case you attempt to do that on the sly, or are persuaded by the employer to work sitting on the other side of the table or from home, the risk is always there that the immigration authorities would come to know of it, or be informed about it, and take action against you for violation of the visa rules. If that unfortunately comes to pass, you run the risk of arrest and/or deportation. Further, you may never be allowed to enter that country again.

iv) Another point to note is that it could take three months *or more* to procure a 'work permit'. In other words, depending on the period for which it has been issued in the first place, your 'tourist visa' *could* expire before a 'work permit' is due to be issued (if at all!). Consider the consequences if your work permit is still awaited, the 'tourist' visa is set to expire in the meanwhile, and (worst still) if it is not renewed or extended any further. Over and above that, if you are about to run out of funds.

At the mercy of the employer

Then you have a choice of staying on within the country, obviously illegally, relying solely on the assurances and promises of your employer (that things will be taken care of, or that the 'work permit' would come by very shortly), and risk your future. The employer would naturally be taking advantage of the situation that you'd find yourself in. Realizing that you could be in serious trouble in a foreign land, with no friend to stand by you, you may try to convince yourself that your prospective employer would deliver as promised.

What you need to understand is that, under such eventualities, he would have you completely under his control and at his mercy. You would have nowhere to go because your visa would have expired by then. You would be what is commonly termed as an 'illegal alien'. You cannot leave because you have no proper visa stamp on your passport, or till your stay has been regularized somehow or the other (i.e., the tourist visa is extended, or your work permit does come through finally)!

Staying out of trouble

Would you like to risk ending up in such a situation? I am sure you wouldn't.

As I said earlier, a tourist visa is adequate for the purpose of *gaining* entry to a country, but *not for taking up a job*. A few (but, do note, very few) countries in Africa are not *that* strict about working without a work-permit, as long as it can be shown that an application has *actually been submitted* to the proper authorities. As far as *you* are concerned, being new to that country, how would you know whether, and to what extent, you should rely on an assurance to that effect? At best, it would remain a grey area. Therefore, the possibility remains that you *could* get into deep trouble if the authorities happen to catch you working anywhere without the necessary permit in your possession.

It may all depend (or, so would the employer claim!) on the 'contacts' or the 'influence' that he may have at the right places. How sure could you be about that? Again, it can take you only that far, and leave you open to serious risks including a jail term and/or an ignominious deportation.

To trust him on his assurance or to wait till the 'permit' is actually in your hands – the choice, if there is really any, is yours. But everything said and done, and after having an idea of what could be the 'downside' and its implications, jumping the gun could be fraught with grave risks, injurious to your health and well-being, so better avoided.

If you *have* to go for it

If, for whatever reason, being left with no better choice, or out of sheer compulsion, or for personal reasons, you decide that you *must take up the job offered* under the circumstances mentioned above, and would like to report for duty at the earliest, you have very few options left.

Under such circumstances, I can only suggest that you have a return ticket handy, and perform your tasks for a limited period only, without making the fact (that you are 'working') apparent or obvious to others locally, and letting only the minimum number of people know about it (if that is *ever* possible! Nobody is a fool, you know!). Additionally, it is advisable to stay away from your supposed office desk (may be, work from home or hotel) till the 'permit' is received.

But for how long? You will have only the employer's assurance and his promise to go by, while the clock ticks, the countdown continues, and the 'tourist visa' is nearing expiry. That's back to square one, I am afraid.

The 'alarm bells'

I referred earlier to 'alarm bells'. Let me explain the reason for saying that. The fact is, immediately after your selection it takes but only a few days and some routine formalities (he would surely have employed expatriates before!) for the employer to apply for a work permit. In fairness, he ought to do that immediately after your appointment is finalized, because the visa could take three months or more for issue, as it happens quite often. If he chooses to delay initiating action, he knows that, in effect, he is running the risk of *delaying* having you formally on board.

The obvious question that would beg an answer would be: "If he is in so great a hurry to have you on board and for you to start work with his organisation, what stopped him from submitting an application to the immigration authorities soon after selection?

Shouldn't he have done that right away! What was he waiting for?"

If the prospective employer only makes promises, insists that you first make the trip all the way, but takes no action to apply to the immigration authorities for your 'work permit', there can be no logical explanation for the delay. Under such circumstances, one can only consider it as a 'red flag', be on guard and not commit oneself. The possible dangers were highlighted earlier, and are also presented in the next section of this chapter.

Suggested precautions

Having said all that, still if you have to go and join, I can only suggest that you leave your homeland only after obtaining a copy of the application along with evidence that your (prospective) employer has paid the necessary fees towards the same and has indeed applied for the 'work permit'.

For the rest, defer all celebrations for later, trust your luck, and keep your return ticket handy.

Oh yes, also keep your fingers crossed and do not forget to pray! Because, if you decide to leave without a formal 'work permit' in hand, there could be other problems that you might face that I take no great pleasure in narrating, but which you should be aware of.

[A small suggestion: If you get put off by the above, please take heart. The risks described above are not about African countries alone. These are true for many countries around the world. Unscrupulous elements and unethical employers abound in all corners of the globe. Whether you are negotiating with someone in Africa, the Middle East, or South East Asia, or Europe etc., it is important to be well-informed and equipped with the required information to (at least) be able to identify the minefields or the red flags when you happen to come across them. For all you know, none of the problems of the nature outlined above may come your way. In the end, things may work out smoothly and entirely to your satisfaction.]

Hold on to your passport

Quite a few employers on the pretext of applying for a 'working visa' may ask for and take away your passport after you have landed in his country. Later, they would cook up many excuses for not giving it back early enough. Neither would they show you evidence that they have actually applied for a 'work permit'.

It happens in Africa, it happens in the Middle East, it happens in many places. Why do they do that? The reasons could be one or all of the following:

a. The employer may want to make sure that you do not desert him or his organisation at your whim and fancy.

b. He may be aiming to save on the permit fees.

c. He may also like to maintain secrecy about the number of expatriates on his work-force.

d. In the process he may be saving on taxes and employee benefits.

e. He also holds an employee to ransom as he can, if he so chooses, inform the authorities at any time if he is upset with the employee. Remember that the unfortunate employee *cannot leave the country without the passport*.

The most important thing to remember, therefore, is *not* to lose possession of your passport, but to hang on to it for dear life at all times. Talk with your colleagues, enquire in the market. Find out the true state of affairs. If your colleagues do not have their passports with them, or the market report about your organization is discouraging, make up your mind as to whether you'd like to stay on to work for such an organisation, or like to retain the right to leave that country when you please (or have to!).

To avoid unpleasantness, when the time comes to produce your passport for any official formalities, you may yourself like to go to the immigration office with it, get the visa stamped, and come back with the passport still safely in your possession.

A point to be noted here. Under the circumstances described above, if things fall apart, contracts entered into with the employer do not have much practical significance or enforceability. Hence, the choice of the right employer is of great importance. As is evident, while going to a new place, the chips could be stacked against you if you do not take an informed decision but rush into things. At the end of the day, it all depends on how fortunate you have been and how good your employer happens to be.[4]

---

[4] Refer also to Chapter V on this subject.

Legal action is not an option

f.   If the 'work permit' is prematurely withdrawn or cancelled at the instance of your employer, pursuing legal action to enforce the contract becomes difficult, if not impossible, because:

g.   Without a valid 'visa', the aggrieved employee is no longer able to live in the country concerned. Without your employer's sponsorship, you cannot obtain a visa anyway (unless you leave the country and re-enter as a tourist).

h.   The employer – being based locally – is in a much better position compared to the expatriate who is there temporarily on an assignment and hardly has a 'base' of his own;

i.   The aggrieved employee may not have the required 'means' or 'resources' (I have consciously put the two foregoing words within quotation marks) to out-gun his employer.

j.   The cost – to sustain oneself, and pay the legal fees – can be prohibitive.

Let's be clear about it. If the 'working visa' is withdrawn suddenly, or you fall out with your employer, or get disillusioned after arrival, you may have no option but to pack your bags, leave the country and come back home in a jiffy.

Quitting and leaving – not easy

But that is not why you took all the trouble to go over there! The trip was *not* to be back among your relatives and friends in your own country in quick time. Apart from all the inconveniences, and the costs involved, coming back home could be embarrassing for many reasons.

i)   For one, you would have, most likely, left a job in India to go to Africa. You may not get that old job, or your old position in that organization, back that easily, if at all.

ii)   Secondly, if it was your very first trip abroad, you may have told the whole world, and rejoiced with all of them, upon your good luck. It would be extremely embarrassing for you and your family to return home in no time flat, with nothing to show for your efforts.

iii)   Even after your return, getting a new job may not be exactly a cake-walk, rather extremely difficult. It is always much easier to find another job, if you already have a job in hand. It would help greatly in relocating, if you are professionally well-qualified. Otherwise, it could be a bit of a problem. (More about this later).

iv) There are many who cannot even afford the return fare home. Further, they may have no savings to keep the home fire burning till another job is found. They may actually have nothing to come back to! So perforce, they must stay back, accept whatever hand-outs come their way, live from hand to mouth, and hope for the nightmare to go away some day, and for better times to come. Caught between a rock and a hard place, it can be a pitiable and a painful situation, and a very sorry state of affairs indeed – believe me. I have seen a few in that position, hence these words of caution.

Career prospects back home

In addition to the above, there are a few other issues that you need to keep in mind:

i) Although the pay packet is generally quite good, the experience gained in Africa is rarely considered a value-addition to your own C.V.

In the minds of those employers in India the African experience does not count for much, or is considered to add to your market value by way of 'overseas or foreign exposure'. In fact, your market value may slip since, in their perception, you may have actually *fallen behind* and missed out on 'progress'. (Don't be surprised if I tell you that their assumptions *may* have some basis.)

ii)   The longer you stay away from your home territory, the more you lose contacts with the markets back home. The 'out of sight, out of mind' syndrome acts here too, and the market will forget about you in no time flat. On your return, getting back into circulation and to land another job quickly could prove to be that much more difficult. If you plan to be back home looking for a job in a few years' time, you should keep this factor in mind and, in the least, keep your old contacts alive.

iii)   On the personal front, you could become an alien in your homeland. During your absence from India, life would have moved on for your friends, business associates and valuable (past) contacts. They would have restructured their lives and learnt, by and by, to continue without you. If and when you decide to return, you would actually be out of their loop, no longer a part of their universe, and may find it quite a problem getting back into their orbit, or *any* orbit for that matter. The old equations, and the old magic, may not be there at all. On the contrary, *you* may be the one who would find it difficult to relate, to reconnect, to catch up with the world you left behind. Remember, times change, and some people change with them. You may have to start afresh trying to rebuild your life. Let me tell you – it will not be easy.

Wrapping up

Hence, complete all your homework *before* you take off for the great blue yonder. Plan long term. Once you land in Africa, and with good luck land on your feet, endeavour to stay there as long as you can. If you are fortunate, the stay could turn out to be a 'rewarding' experience in more ways than one!

Obtaining a citizenship is another way of getting rid of the continued uncertainties, the underbelly of tension, and avoiding the risks inherent in a 'work permit' regime. Many people I know have taken that route, have decided to put in their roots in the countries of their choice, and lived happily ever after.

Quite a few others have made their money, sent their children abroad for higher studies, and yet kept pining for the good old 'motherland'. After some soul searching and weighing the options, some have packed their bags and come back 'home' to the land of their birth.

CHAPTER IV

LANDING ON YOUR FEET

Don't burn your bridges

The key, therefore, is to make sure that you land on your feet. While you are busy planning your trip abroad, let's take a moment to talk about risk management. Consider not burning your bridges, consider leaving the back door or an exit route open (remember Abhimanyu in the classic Mahabharat?) *if* things go wrong after you land at your new destination. How do you manage the risks?

[I reported for duty to take over as the managing director of a bank in Africa, only to find within the first hour that the bank was under moratorium ordered by their Central bank. This fact had not been revealed by their honourable chairman and owner when he had interviewed me for the job.]

Let me note down here my 'tuppence worth', and hope that – at the end of the day – *you don't need my advice.*

If you are already employed, try to take a long leave from your present employer and report for the new job overseas. Make up your mind as quickly as possible. If you like your new job, feel comfortable with what you see at first hand, make a quick trip back home, meet your (soon to be 'former') employer, and offer your resignation. The notice period could be a factor to be sorted out if you take this route.

The risk

This process, of course, carries an element of risk which you should be aware of. Firstly, you are not supposed to hold two jobs at the same time-unless (rarely) permitted by the employers concerned. Secondly, if the new employer makes an early reference with your immediately preceding employer, and comes to know that, till then, you have not resigned from your previous job, your future plans could tumble like a house of cards.

You may consider mailing your resignation from overseas. Avoid this option if you can. If you take recourse to this, you run the risk of upsetting your (former) employer and spoiling a working relationship which could, someday, work to your advantage. For example, you may yet need a good reference from your immediate past employer. Terminal settlements could also be delayed. As the saying goes: "Never bang a door shut, you may have to go back".

A better option

It would be the best if, right in the beginning, you can take your present employer, or your immediate boss, into confidence, tell him what you are up to, seek his cooperation (blessing), take his advice as to your best course of action, and go by his advice. Note to keep him posted about developments. It always pays to have your boss on your side.

The best course of action in my opinion would be to keep things as transparent and above-board as possible at all times. It would, of course, depend on the type of organisation and the rapport that you have with your present superiors.

Make an exploratory trip

For senior level assignments, you may be offered an option by the prospective employer in Africa to visit the country and see the new organization for yourself first-hand. The fact-finding mission is usually arranged to provide the prospective employee a sense of comfort, and help him make up his mind. Since the offer comes from the employer-to-be, they are happy to pay for the short round-trip. The trip also gives an opportunity to the organisation's top-level people to meet with the new entrant, and help increase the overall comfort level.

Since you are first time visitor to a new continent, and a completely alien country, your request for an initial visit may not be taken amiss by a decent employer. You can be frank about your doubts and uncertainties. You can also tell them that you'd resign from your old job only after your familiarization trip. This will make 'reference to the past employer' that much above-board.

The trip will give you an opportunity not only to know a bit about the new country and the organization you plan to join, but also give you a feel of the place, a choice of where to stay, the shops, the general facilities and transport, the availability of schools for your children, food and restaurants, recreation and life style etc. Your spouse will have a million questions – so carry a questionnaire from him/her to make your life easier.

Research and Homework Important

The above would, obviously, be the best possible option. However, if you are fortunate enough to have this option available to you, you may still need to go through this book to know what questions to ask during the several rounds of interviews, and what to look out for when you have arrived at the new place.

Generally, the advantage of an exploratory or familiarization trip is not available to most. Under such circumstances, please make sure that you do your homework and your research, find out all you can and all that you need to know, ask all the right questions during your interview and after (this book should be helpful in your mission), and only then make up your mind whether to take up the offer.

I know of people who have joined organizations in Africa, stayed for about a week, had a taste of the new culture, the new place, got scared when they heard about the security risks (these could come as a great shock initially, trust me), and simply disappeared in no time flat never to be back ever again.

> *[It happened to a team of IT guys representing a top-of-the-line Indian IT firm visiting Nairobi. On the very first evening of their visit, they were mugged on their walk back home. The experience was so traumatic that the entire team was gone by the next morning.]*

Displacing spouse or family

If you have a family, do not take them on your first trip out. Leave them behind for about the first six months or so. I know about the cost of two establishments, and the spouse having to manage everything without your help; but this is a better option for the first-time visitor to a new country. See the place for yourself, and take a decision when you grow in your comfort level.

If your spouse is working you may wish to let your spouse continue in employment – even if it means a separation and disruption in family life. Remember, as with any new country, life in Africa could be full of uncertainties, and developments beyond your or your employer's control. Things do happen that *can* cut short your African honeymoon. (I cannot help it but keep it vague for good reasons. Ask me when you meet me!)

It is important that the other spouse retains the job in hand. This is of utmost importance if the job is a good one, and too good to give up without any compelling reason. If your spouse continues to work and earn while you are away it could tremendously increase your risk-taking ability as well as peace of mind of the family as a whole. Decisions taken on an impulse should be avoided.

Earn in Africa, spend in India

It is always a better option to earn in Africa, and spend in India. The difference in the salary levels, and the fact that you will be spending only on your maintenance and not for your entire family (including children's education and medical facilities — both could be prohibitively expensive), will provide you with a better opportunity for saving. Separation for a few years would be well worth it. The income level would also make it possible for a couple of trips back and forth without pinching your bank balance too much.

If you have a working spouse back home, the option would still be available to you to leave your job in Africa (if you are forced to), or for your spouse to leave his/her job in India (if it is worth the sacrifice) and join you in Africa. The options will always be available to you to exercise at your convenience.

A family life

Having said that, I will now go ahead and contradict myself. If things do work out in your favour, it is a better option in the long run for the family to be together than live separately for months or years. The stress factor associated with living alone will start telling on you and your spouse and, in all probability, *will* force a decision at some point in time. Be ready for it.

Why go abroad, why go to Africa at all!

If you have been patient enough to read up to this point, it's about time when you start wondering: given the above scenario, why on earth should one look for a job in Africa?

My purpose, as I said earlier, is not to discourage you, nor to paint a negative picture of those lovely places and the best of employers in Africa, but help you make an informed choice. Everything that I have written in the foregoing paragraphs is borne out of my close encounters (not all of them pleasant ones) of myself and of my friends in Africa. But everything said and done, I did have a great time in Africa, and I'd love to go there again. There is no reason why you should not enjoy working and living there too.

Having said all that, the important thing is to land on your feet. That is, to find a good job, end up with a decent employer, have a pleasant work environment and enjoy life. It is easier said than done, but to do otherwise would mean 'trouble'. The next chapter provides a few guidelines to help you avoid 'trouble'. Therefore, read on.

CHAPTER V

THE EMPLOYER

In Africa, like anywhere else in the world, the range of employers will be wide – from private, entrepreneurial ventures to multinationals. Knowing your employer is as important as the oft-repeated saying: 'know your customer'. This factor is of critical importance because your new employer will be the one acting as your 'sponsor' to obtain the 'working visa' for you. The continuation of your stay in the foreign country will depend on the continuity of his sponsorship.

For all the above reasons and more, it is wiser to do a little bit of research to make sure that you have picked a winning card instead of a bad one. But wait! Let us first understand as to who could be a bad employer, and why?

Landing on a banana skin

Let me offer a few samples of what you may discover on arrival at your new job. Yes, as is my wont, here are all the 'bad' things that you might find.

a.   The assignment may turn out to be something completely different from that pictured to you during the selection process.

b.   The job profile, your designation, or the person you are supposed to report to, may change to your detriment.

c.   The work culture may go against your grain.

d.   The company may not be of the type projected to you during the interview.

e.   It may not turn out to be of good repute.

f.   The facilities provided may not be to your liking or far different from that promised.

g.   You may find that the salary offered is severely understated vis-à-vis what had been indicated or agreed earlier. It may also be significantly less as compared to your peers.

h.   They may not pay your salary at all. Or pay only a small fraction of that promised.

Yes, any (or all) of the above is possible if you happen to be out of luck. Remember that once you land you are at the mercy of your 'sponsor' in a foreign country, dependent on that 'work permit' to be able to stay and work there for your living. The matter of ending up with a good organization is, therefore, critical.

Research helps

Since you are a first-time visitor to the African continent, you may not have the necessary contacts to do good research on the organization offering you employment. It would be great if you knew whom to ask, or get some answers from one you trust. The options are, indeed, few for a new visitor. For middle or junior level positions, you really cannot do much. So take the necessary insurance – as advised earlier, and try out your luck.

I suggest that, among other avenues of research, the local High Commission or Embassy could be a very good bet. They would usually be in a position to provide some help with regard to your queries about the desirability of the organisation as an 'ideal' employer. They are mostly very informative and helpful.

Fact-finding mission

For those going on senior or top-level assignments, they may be offered a familiarisation tour to the country concerned – before they sign on the dotted line. Accept the offer, make a trip to see things for yourself, and then decide. Do not forget to drop in at the local consulate or embassy and check out with the people there (the commercial attaché or someone similar) while you are on a visit to the country of your future employment. Their inputs could help you to take that final decision, and may stand you in good stead in the long run.

CHAPTER VI

COMENSATION PACKAGE

This is the "Aha!" moment, the bottom line, the great motivator, and one of the most important issues on top of our minds when we think of migrating. The issues may be summed up in five words: would it be worth it? A few items of interest out of this author's experience are laid out here to help you on your way:

Obtain a written contract

For whatever it is worth, get a duly signed, written letter of offer followed by a written contract. The terms of employment should find mention in complete detail in the document. If nothing else, it will serve as an 'aid memoir' and a permanent record of your entitlements, and help to avoid disputes in future.

Salary in foreign currency or …?

Given an option how would you like to draw your salary – in local currency, or in US$? Many corporations, even smaller companies and business establishments in some of the countries in Africa are open to – and may even offer you the option of – payment of compensation packages in foreign currencies of choice, directly credited to your overseas bank account. There are several reasons for that, among which are:

    a.   the political stability of the host country

    b.   Idi Amin-like (Uganda) situation happening

    c.   stable exchange rate

    d.   repatriation convenience

The exchange rate problem and other issues

Let us look at the options, the pros and cons:

i)   If a currency depreciates, you can do nothing about it but try your best and plan in advance to protect your net earnings in terms of your home currency. Exchange rates can vary and they do – sometimes very wildly too – for strange reasons.

ii)   In many countries of the sub-Saharan Africa, the US$ is as commonly used as the local currency. In some countries there are innumerable exchange bureaus at every place. (You will hardly find an exchange bureau easily in South Africa, though! Change your money to Rand before you go for your trip to S.A.). Prices for hotels, visa fees, air fare, tourist taxis, room rents, routine services etc. are freely quoted in (for example) Shilling as in US$.

iii)   Even before you can have access to a money changing bureaux you may need some cash for local expenses (like cab fare, tips). Better to carry some small change in notes and coins before your departure.

iv)   If the salary has been determined in a local currency, there is a possibility that, down the line, you may end up with the net take home pay (in terms of your home currency) that is less than what you started with.

v)   Try to negotiate for your salary to be fixed, and paid for the most part, in US$. This step will protect – if not enhance – your net pay packet in terms of your home currency. This scenario may relatively be a more acceptable scenario than the wild fluctuations that one may witness with currencies of some of the African or a few of the South or Central American countries. Such unfortunate turn of events could leave you with a very weak local currency and consequently a severely depleted pay packet.

Repatriation

Find out about the facilities and the procedure to remit (or repatriate) what you earn out of the country where you are based. This information should be collected from your prospective employer at the time of negotiation of your compensation package. After all, you are going to a foreign land, taking a degree of risk, to earn and enjoy your income at home. That's what most people look forward to. Hence the enquiries about repatriation facilities are essential and necessary.

Some of the countries have liberalized their exchange rates completely. There, it is extremely easy to open a bank account in US$ or any major foreign currency of choice, convert and reconvert from one currency to another, remit any amount for any sort of payment overseas etc. No questions asked as long as no money laundering or an illegal activity is involved.

For some countries, only the non-residents are given free transfer facilities.

In others, like Ethiopia, where (as of now) the balance of payment if negative and foreign exchange is scarce, it is quite difficult to repatriate your income in foreign exchange. The formalities are quite cumbersome too. (The scenario has changed for the better since then. See a thumb-nail report of 2014 later in this book. The way things were going then, in 2025, things may be even better; do check them out.)

Salary – cost to company, gross, net, net of taxes?

There are several ways in which a company may structure their compensation packages. For the sake of clarity, and as far as possible, negotiate the amount you will earn in terms of 'net of taxes'. The reason is that – being a complete stranger – you will have no idea whatsoever as to the tax structure in that country. Even if the salary is quoted on a pre-tax basis, *request that the post-tax amount is advised to you* by them. This will help you to have a better fix on the actual amount that you are likely to earn while in employment with the company.

Find out the perks that go with your position. Find out the amount of tax that you will be called upon to pay towards them. It should be included in the above calculation and netted off as stated just above.

On the books, off the books

A few organizations may tell you that they will pay part of the amount on their books. The rest will be paid 'off the books' – paid either in cash locally, or in US$ through an overseas account/bank. Even multinationals do that. If not declared to the proper local authorities or properly reflected in the books of accounts, this mode helps only the employer to avoid taxes. For you the risks are as follows:

i)   If the arrangement is *actually* shown in the contract, but not approved by the authorities, you may get caught in the cross-fires if any action is taken against your employer on this ground.

ii) If the amount payable is 'off the books', it is most likely that it will not be mentioned in the contract either. Later, in case of disputes and claims, it may become extremely difficult for you to *prove* to anyone what was the actual salary mutually agreed upon and payable to you. Try to obtain a side-letter confirming the arrangement, if you can.

iii) The amount that is 'off the books' is not supposed to be paid to you as at the end of every month during routine salary payment. Separate 'arrangements' would be required to be put in place to meet the situation. It may so happen that every month you may have to approach the 'boss', or the owner of the company, or the head of accounts, by way of a gentle reminder for the amount that is payable to you 'off the books'. That routine by itself could be embarrassing. It may become even more embarrassing if the payment of this sum gets delayed every month, and is released only after reminders.

Hazards associated with payment of salary 'off the books'

What could be even worse would be the situation where the portion payable 'off-the-books' – in US$ or in local currency – is not paid promptly on the due dates every month but is allowed to accumulate. Remember, you can only remind, pursue and press up to a point for payment of your dues. You know that, and 'they' too know that.

Pressed too hard, I have seen such unscrupulous employers taking recourse to paying only a small portion of the total (by then substantial) accumulated dues to keep the person off their backs – till the next due date. With the net dues mounting every month, quite understandably it becomes next to impossible for one to sacrifice one's hard-earned savings, cut one's losses and walk away from the job. Most of the time a person faced with such a situation and mounting 'receivables', willy-nilly stays on, hoping against hope that someday....! In the end, if he is fortunate, he may recover a significant portion of his dues. But what if he is not so fortunate? Being unable to subsist in that country any further on his savings, being finally being convinced that the dues perforce have to be given up, foregone for good, he would be forced to quit in frustration and disgust.

No risk with reputed companies

The risks outlined above obviously do not apply the reputed employers including the respected, long established business houses, corporations or multinationals. You could verify things on your own from the Net and from your acquaintances, sign on the dotted line and enjoy life. If the payment details are 'on the books', the payment to your account would automatically be processed by the accounts dept. along with all others'. Where the company is privately owned, or not so well known, a little bit of research about its track record can do no harm.

Medical Insurance

The cost of medicines and hospitalization overseas is prohibitive anywhere – including in the African continent. *Make sure that medical insurance cover is provided by the prospective employer for yourself and your family members.* The medical insurance should ideally cover reimbursement of all expenses towards hospitalization, if not also for reimbursement (against production of bills/ receipts) of doctors' consultation fees (outside the hospital) and towards the medicines purchased locally even without hospitalisation.

Children's education

If you plan to relocate your school-going children to Africa, think about the cost of education, especially the school fees. This too is usually very high everywhere and will take away a substantial portion of your income. Negotiate, if you can, for reimbursement of school fees, including admission and examination fees. Include this in the contract. If you hope to stay longer, the reimbursement should include education for two children up to the college level. Note that these could be taxed too.

Vehicle / conveyance

If there is room for negotiation ask for a car, or at least a loan to buy a new or second-hand car. Owing to the risks involved, a car is a necessity in most of the African countries. It is not a luxury. In some places, it is risky to walk even short distances to the nearest shopping mall at (any) odd hours – especially after dark. (More on this later.)

The other perks

These depend on the level at which you are joining. Most expatriate benefits include onward (at the time of joining duty) and return fares after the end of contract, for the entire family. Find out the 'class' of travel being offered to you. It could be 'club class' or first class too. If not included in the contract, the income tax authorities in certain countries tend to value this as perks and levy taxes on this item as an extra benefit. (Some places have a rule that anything not included in black and white in the contract will be deemed to be perquisites, and will be taxed accordingly. Therefore, beware and ask for details.)

As you can well understand, before you go overboard with the 'perks' that you have been able to extract as part of your contract, find out how these 'perks' are treated locally for the purpose of taxation, affecting your net take-home pay. Sometimes, these could hit you badly.

Just to illustrate the point: I was offered a choice between a new car and one that was with my employer for about three years – both were Mercedes. Since I was asked, I had no reason not to opt for a new car But then, I was gently advised that the value of 'perks' would be computed based on the price of the new car – even if it was 'company owned' and allotted to me only for official use. I changed my mind very quickly and opted for the older Mercedes.

On another occasion I was politely told that travelling by air to and from Africa by any class other than 'first class' was not an option, even if I was not travelling on official business. I was advised that if I *did* travel by any other class, there was every possibility of it being noticed by others. This was likely to hurt the image of my employer ("Our CEOs are given only the best!"), hence 'avoid'.

CHAPTER VII

IN YOUR OWN INTEREST

A few pieces of free, unsolicited advice for your better health:

1. Maintain a low profile and, most important, just mind your own business. Doing so is for your own good.

2. Do not get involved in local politics, or in discussions about the host government or its policies. Remember that you do not enjoy the same rights or privileges as a citizen otherwise may.

3.   Do not do anything to abuse the hospitality or the sensitivity of the host country or its people. You are a guest there.

4.   If you do not know how to drive, learn. Do this immediately when you get to realise that you *may* be going there. Get your driving licence *well before* you leave your home country. This applies both to you and to your spouse. Just before leaving for your new destination, obtain an international driving licence (it is valid for a year from the date of issue). Obtain a local licence as soon as you can do so after arrival. Carry your home country driving licence with you too. It helps you to obtain a local one once you are there.

5.   Even if you are entitled to a driver, or appoint one of your own, he would be going home in the evening at the end of his duty hours. Normally, they live on the outskirts and depend on public transport to commute from residence to their workplace. Hence, most cannot stay back till late. In some countries they are very particular about their entitlement to a day's leave once a week. So, you may have to take

the steering wheel on your way back home if you decide to stay late at the office.

Social engagements late in the evening or over the weekends may also warrant driving around town without the assistance of your faithful driver. If the family has to manage with only one car, then many a times, you may have to drop your spouse at office and go about your business thereafter – driving around on your own. Whichever way you look at it, it is advisable to learn how to drive if you don't yet know how to.

6.   Carry your driving licence with you while leaving your home country. In addition, remember to take out an international driving licence before departure. There is a limit to the validity of international driving licences. Procure a local driving licence as soon as possible.

7.   The local driving licence (DL) acts as your ID at many places, especially when you go around as a tourist. The DL will save you a lot of money by way of entry fees at reserve forests and national parks (at many places

around the world it is relatively quite high for foreigners), and make life easier for you wherever you need to show an ID.

8.   A few words about driving habits, road manners, patience and common courtesies while at the steering wheel. Some of these will be seem to be 'strange' or ridiculous to people from the Indian subcontinent, but let me assure you the road manners that I wish to highlight below are not out-of-the-world. They are practised by all developed societies round the world. And they work, they really do! So, here goes:

   a. Left hand drive or right hand? It depends on which country had colonized that part of Africa. If it's the British, places like Tanganyika (now Tanzania, Kenya, Uganda) then you have a right-hand drive system. If it's the West-African region, colonised by the French or the Belgians, then you have to get used to left-hand drive.

   b. This means, in a country with the right-hand rule, you are to strictly observe the norm that the car from your right has the right of way. Whatever the circumstances, whichever road you are on – even if you're on the main thoroughfare and the other car is coming from the side road, or you are at a roundabout – you must slow down or stop and give way to the car arriving from your right. Break this rule at your own risk, apart from the possibility of an accident.

Every country has its own conventions, protocols, culture and peculiarities as far as driving practices are concerned. When you land in a new country and intend to acquire a driving licence, first get to know, in absolutely clear terms, their local driving practices. Only then take up the steering wheel. It would cause you no harm if you occupy the passenger seat or have some local 'driver' next to you for the first few days to break you in and observe what he does.

c. While on the subject of driving, do remember that the horn in your car is not meant for honking. My dear fellow Indians, believe me when I say that it *is* possible to drive through a crowded road without blowing your horn even once. If I could have, surely you can, too. Not only abroad, but in India itself. It *is* possible. Like many developed countries in the west, in most of the African countries too, it is the height of bad manners to honk. If another driver has done something very offensive, e.g. cut into your lane without adequate notice or signal (that is considered offensive – I am not pulling your leg!), just a short toot or a smart tap of your horn directed at the offending driver to indicate your displeasure is enough to make him cringe and apologise to you for his bad behaviour.

Once, in Calcutta, I took a cab during office hours from my home to the central business district about 12 kilometres away. The roads were crowded. However, I began to notice that the driver never used the horn – not even at places where a Calcutta cab driver would absolutely have. He drove the entire length without using the hooter in his car even once. While paying him off at the end of the journey, I complimented him for it. He set the record straight, explaining to me that the mechanism went out of order the previous night after a heavy shower, and that he had found no time to fix it yet. However, it only proved the point that using the horn even in a city like Calcutta was very much possible. Patience is the key.

d. Another suggestion is to make the best use of the rear view and the side view mirrors in your vehicle. Hand signals are not welcome. Waving wildly to signal to the other drivers will make no sense. The mirrors are meant to used, so *use* them to navigate.

e. Remember to thank another for all services rendered – big or small. Saying 'please' and 'thank you' should be as automatic or unconscious a habit as breathing. Show that you actually *mean it*. If you are at the steering wheel, and a watchman opens the gates for you, or you pass by a watchman or security guard on duty, do not forget to offer your thanks or show your appreciation for the services rendered by a short wave of your palm. On the road, if a car ahead of you moves to one side of the road to clear the way for you, or to allow you to overtake him, do not take that courtesy for granted. Acknowledge the consideration shown to you and the courtesy by a wave of your hand. He will wave back in return.

9.   More on road manners: Do not force your way into another lane or in front of another vehicle. Learn to be patient. At the first opportunity one of the other cars will slow down, if not stop altogether, and signal to you to tell you that you can have your way. It is not fiction, but plain and simple good manners. If you wish to cross the road, an oncoming car will stop and the driver would signal to you and allow you to cross the road, before he moves on once again. (You do not have to go too far to see it yourself, just visit Dubai or any place in Europe). If you are trying to reverse your car – say while parking, taking your car out of the

parking lot or while turning into a driveway –
the cars that you happen to block or hold up
would wait patiently and courteously till you
have completed your manoeuvres. Not a
single driver anywhere would give a blast on
the horn to hurry you up or show his
impatience. On every such occasion after you
have completed your manoeuvres, do
remember to acknowledge the courtesy shown
and thank them for their patience.

Yellow fever Injection

10. Check if you require to produce this certificate
while departing from or coming back to India. It
may depend on your destination, but for travel
to any part of Africa it is a must. Take a yellow
fever injection at least two weeks (verify this
time period in advance for the latest applicable
rules) before the date of departure (the lead
time for the injection to start working is said to
be 10 days). Do not forget to obtain a certificate
for the injection taken. The effect of the
injection is said to last for ten years. The
certificate, therefore, is supposed to remain
valid also for ten years. In order to preserve it

for ten years, it is advisable to have it laminated.

Carry it together with your passport at all times – especially when re-entering India – or traveling to other countries in Europe or the Americas. You could be quarantined for several days if you are not able to produce the yellow-fever certificate at the point of entry. So, be warned! Keeping the passport and the yellow fever certificate together at all times would be a good idea.

Buy a round-trip ticket

11.   International carriers usually issue 'return tickets', not one-way tickets, as a matter of routine. Of course, you can procure a one-way ticket if you want to, but for that you may have to make a specific request. While planning your trip overseas, it is advisable to buy a return ticket (with a six-month or a one-year option, though it might cost you a little more than one with a shorter life-span). The return ticket can be held for your travel during your annual leave, thus saving you a considerable sum. The return (i.e. two-way) fare for

international travel is sometimes almost equal or very marginally more than a one-way fare. Hence, as matter of routine most people buy a 'return ticket', even if they intend not to use that portion of the ticket, and allow the 'return' leg of the ticket to lapse unutilized.

12.   There is another advantage of buying a return ticket that I must mention. If (God forbid) you have to leave your place where you are employed at very short notice, the return ticket will come to your help, and save you from buying another, far costlier, one-way ticket home (provided you still have enough funds to pay for it). Keep the ticket with the passport at all times – easily accessible at short notice. The reasons for this bit of advice will become apparent sometimes later.

Workers' rights

13.   Thinking of appointing a helping hand? In several countries, the blue-collared workers (including your watchman, house-girl/maid, driver, gardener, etc.) are organised, have quite a few well-defined rights, including leave entitlements, and are very particular about

them. In some places they have very strong industrial associations, which can cause a lot of problems for you if you, as their employer, step out of line. This matter about how you treat and interact with your domestic employees must be handled with extreme care and tact. It also has other implications (which I am unable to articulate right now). So ask the older residents as to the norms and practices applicable to the people of that place before you engage someone.

CHAPTER VIII

WHAT'S AVAILABLE, WHAT'S NOT

Shopping complexes, department stores

Major cities like Harare, Dar-es-Salam, Lagos, Kampala, Johannesburg or Cape Town have large department stores and shopping complexes where virtually every item of daily necessity (and beyond) is available. There are many shops and stores which are run by Asians (Indians, Pakistanis etc.) that specifically cater to Indian tastes. So, buying your favourite curry powder etc. may not pose a problem everywhere. Once you get to know the place, the nooks and corners, you will be able find your way around and select your favourite joints in no time.

In fact, cities like Nairobi, Dar-es-Salam, Mombasa are so full of Indian stores and restaurants that, even for a moment, you will not feel that you have left the Indian shores.

Imported goods

Several of these countries (except South Africa) have relatively narrow manufacturing bases, so they have to import most of the major items of daily necessity – from pencils, erasers to kitchenware and cars. Actually, you will be spoilt for choice – so many **'foreign' goods** are so easily available there that your approach to shopping will undergo a sea-change over the months, without your even being conscious about the change. Frankly speaking, after years of living in Africa, it may prove tough when you finally decide to come back to India to settle down for good.

There are exceptions, though. Ethiopia, for example, is not flush with foreign exchange at the moment (though the situation could change in the future) and so regulates imports strictly. The foreign exchange is auctioned to the general public. Remittance overseas is difficult. A strict record must be maintained of the amount of foreign exchange brought into the country by every visitor, and accounted for at the point of exit (to prevent black markets in foreign currencies). Hence, do find out the applicable exchange control rules when you negotiate for a job.[5]

Clothes – what to carry and what to wear

Take with you only those which are *specific to your needs* or cost the earth locally. These include clothes (sarees, kurtas, shirts and trousers, ties) and other items of personal wear. Bring along your shoes too. They are very costly there.

Buy some impressive *party outfits* and carry them with you. You will need them for those formal gatherings and get-togethers that would constantly keep you busy – especially over the weekends. Carry with you your *smart casuals* too – for home,

---

[5] I wrote this based on information available at the time of writing. As luck would have it, I visited Ethiopia in 2014.and was glad to observe first-hand that the economy of Ethiopia was in a far better shape. It had become an investment destination of choice. Remittance in or out, for example, was not an issue at all. A pen-picture of my observations, even though dated by now, is furnished at the end of this document.

for outdoors, for the frequent safaris, and for the informal get-togethers that are far too many and far too frequent in those parts especially if you happen to hold a senior executive position.

The Bermuda shorts, the Adidas and the Nikes would come in very handy here. During *safaris*, be sure to wear a cap to protect your head, and save your skin with suitable lotions. At an altitude of about 5,500 feet, the sun does shine with greater intensity in the pollution-free environment, and can quite easily affect your exposed body parts.

Imported suits of excellent quality and reputed brands (Yves St. Laurent, Pierre Cardin etc.) are easily available at a very reasonable price at some outlets in the city. Second-hand goods of every description imported from the developed countries have flooded the market and have kept the price level very low indeed. Quality of these second-hand goods, of course, is another matter.

Speaking about suits, as a legacy of British culture everyone wears suits there. That includes the sweepers, drivers, messengers, managers and CEOs. If you are not used to wearing one, get used to it now – especially if the appointment is at a senior level. Learn to knot a tie properly – if that is still a mystery to you. Blame it on occupational hazard!

Shopping opportunities

Believe me when I say that when people from the African continent come to India for short visits – on business or as a tourist, they shop till they drop. (Like the Indians did before liberalisation when they used to visit the US, London, Singapore or Hong Kong. Times have changed, though.)

For that reason, it would be difficult for me to suggest what gift items to bring along when you are visiting home. Some of the imported luxury goods are still not so easily available in India. You could, perhaps, include them in your shopping lists. Cardamom, cinnamon, etc. are of excellent quality and are also very cheap to buy, as are chocolates, coffee and local tea. Kitchenware, perfumes, liqueur are a few of the other items that readily come to my mind.

But above all, the items that you will never get anywhere are the locally handcrafted wood, copper and stone items. These are treasured everywhere, and are excellent as gift items, as wall pieces, for decorations, and to brighten up your home or office.

Designed copper plates, for example, are a rage but you must buy them only from Zimbabwe. Fabulous wooden masks are available in many parts of Africa. Visit the workshops – no, not the ones the (mzungu[6]) tourists are directed to, but the indigenous ones, where the locals go – and see how they magically transform a block of wood to a thing of beauty.

Hence, ask the local residents where you can find them cheap – for generally the rates are graded. The local weekly markets or 'craft villages' are the best places to shop. Avoid tourist spots. The prices vary widely, so do be careful. Prices are extremely low for the local Africans, or if you speak the lingo, a bit higher if they recognise you as a local Asian. Prices jump manifold if they identify you as a total foreigner, new to the place.

A suggestion: take along a local friend who is fluent with the language when you go bargain hunting. Let her do the bargaining, and keep your mouth shut. You may not get the lowest rates, but you won't be

---

[6] In Swahili the word "mzungu" means a foreigner, usually a white person.

ripped off either, which could happen if you are accompanied by a 'mzungu'.

Carrying items of value

DO NOT carry any item of value, or anything that you may regret losing. Do not carry anything that you cannot afford to lose – costly or otherwise. *Make this a golden rule – not to be violated at any cost.* Else you may have to pay a steep price. No jewellery, no diamond wedding rings, no necklaces or gold bangles please. Wear only imitation items. Everyone does, and it is nothing to be ashamed of. But if those imitation items too looks like the real ones, then avoid wearing them outdoors. No point in tempting fate. Therefore, while preparing for your trip to Africa, do not pack any of the above items. Leave all of them behind for use on another day.

Passport photos

For longer stay, carry about 50 passport sized photographs of yourself. Also, the negative for printing additional copies locally if required. Initially, you will need quite a few. You will require passport sized photographs for almost anything and everything, starting with your ID papers, your driving licence and your alien card. Hence, it would be convenient to have a large initial stock handy for use.

Medicines

Medicines and hospitalization cost the earth. The medicines available there in Africa are mostly imported from the developed countries or from South Africa. So most of the brands prescribed in India – carrying Indian trade names – may not match your prescription or be available there. Carry at least a stock to last about six months or more, till you can re-stock or change your prescription.

Do not burden the traveller

People keep shuttling between India and Africa. It is a matter of common practice to announce a trip to India, and act as a courier for all. The person making a round trip will carry letters, gift items of small sizes, other sundry items, and bring back similar items from India. No one minds. The facility works both ways – offered by all, to all. Medicines and other items of urgent need are gladly carried on request by such visitors from India to Africa.

A point to note: since a traveller has to meet the requests of many, you would do him and everyone else a big favour if you do not burden him or her with heavy or large-sized (even if light-weight) packages, or too many items. Many people I know forget the load constraint during air travel (generally only 15 kg on domestic routes in economy class in India, higher for international travel, but do check) or the traveller's own convenience, and callously burden him with large number of items to carry as part of his personal baggage, causing serious problem for the helpful but hapless traveller.

Avoid the postal system to send valuables

Do not use the local postal system to send items of value – including cheques, drafts – from Africa. If you wish to send money, take the help of banks that use secure electronic fund transfer systems. Or, ask your friends planning to go to India to post your letters containing those drafts, cheques etc. only on reaching the Indian shores. It is faster and also safer. As a matter of courtesy to the 'courier' friend of yours, affix proper postage stamps on the mail in advance. And that means keeping a stock of Indian stamps with you at all times.

Bags, suitcases

Soft luggage or moulded plastics? Soft luggage is usually preferred because it weighs less. But around the continent of Africa as elsewhere, a soft luggage offers the tempting possibility of being ripped open quite easily with a sharp knife or blade. Even at the cost of a few extra kilos, you may prefer to use the 'moulded luggage' variety for durability, added safety and security of your belongings. It is an option worth considering, I assure you. Lock it well, shrink-wrap it, if you can, for additional safety.

The total weight allowed for baggage vary from airline to airline, and from season to season. For the economy class, the maximum allowed on an international flight is generally 40 kilogrammes. However, this could be increased at the sole discretion of the airline, to 60 or 80 kgs. If you approach them with your request, before the ticket is issued. Don't bank on it, but it can be done. (I have.)

A point about the hand baggage. Airlines allow only one piece as a rule –with some exceptions (like your make-up case etc.). Since the incidence of 9/11, the rules have become even stricter. Find out what the applicable rules are at the time of your travel. You must follow the rules strictly. Some airlines add the weight of the hand baggage to that of the checked in baggage. The size of the hand-baggage also matters. So, overloading it may not be a good idea.

Find out about these with the airline concerned before you book your tickets.

CHAPTER IX

A FEW USEFUL HINTS

Local language

A large section of the population – especially those living in the larger cities – speak English. So you will get by without much trouble. But take care. Your wife or partner may pick up the local language much faster than you, through the help of her domestic help or the driver. The language problem will surface once you are outside the main cities and towns. Outside the cities, people are not that comfortable with the English language. In many parts of Africa, Swahili, Kiswahili or its variations are more common.

It is always better to learn the local language as quickly as you can. It is really not very difficult to do so, if you put your mind to it. Knowing the language can help you build bridges with the local population rather quickly and easily.

Education

If your child is to continue education in Africa first find out about the schools in the new country, the syllabi, compatibility with the existing curriculum and the time period as also the criteria for admission (your employer may be able to help). Most countries have very good and high-quality schools (though the standards of colleges may not always be to your choice). There are many options – sometimes quite confusing to a first-time visitor. If you plan to send your child to the universities in UK or the USA, the syllabi offered here could prove very useful indeed.

Residence

On arrival, my advice would be to put up in a 'service apartment' before you take a decision as to where to rent a home. Service apartments are very popular in these parts – especially to the migrating staff. These apartments are fully furnished (includes furnished drawing and bedrooms, a fully furnished kitchen with refrigerator, gas and electric oven, microwave) plus cleaning service, part-time maid, TV and telephone. Generally, one or two bed-roomed units of varied standards are available at very convenient locations. Many have laundry service, restaurants, swimming pools and gyms as matters of added convenience.

This arrangement will give you time to decide on the locality where you'd like to reside in future, the school, and other nitty-gritty of life which should be finalized only (in consultation with, and) on the arrival of your spouse.

If and when you rent a house, the furniture – including electrical and electronic items – can be easily purchased second-hand. There is a continual flow of expatriates (especially around Nairobi, since a large number of the NGOs are stationed there) who sell off their household items before they leave. These are generally of good quality, and mostly available at virtually throw-away prices. The list of these used items on offer will be found pasted on the notice boards at most shopping malls. Take your time and check them out.

Embassy

Immediately on arrival, or as soon as is conveniently possible, register yourself with the local Indian consulate, embassy or High Commission. Get involved in their activities, contribute actively and share in their efforts to develop better ties with the host nation.

Do not take this advice lightly. In times of trouble, they could be your best bet for assistance and support. So, make sure they know about you, and have your contact details with them. Usually this involves calling on them to fill out a simple questionnaire. Do it as soon as you can after your arrival.

Entertainment

Options vary from place to place. Some cities and towns have huge shopping complexes, cineplexes, or malls-cum-multiplexes. There are big and well spread out entertainment complexes that one is just beginning to see in India. (Go and see the 'Village Market' or 'Sarit Centre' in Westlands, Nairobi, or some of the complexes in South Africa to understand what I mean). They offer a whole day's entertainment – including food courts, outdoor and indoor games for adults and children, compact cinema houses, shopping malls, health club, bank, etc. – all under one roof. Some places have only tourist options. Everything said and done – there is no reason whatsoever to stay at home during the week-ends. No one does. Go somewhere, *anywhere* –but just GO!

Food

Food of every description is easily available everywhere. Restaurants are aplenty, offering all varieties of Indian, continental, Chinese and Mughlai food. Local vegetable and fish markets will meet practically every domestic need of yours. And then there are the department stores, shopping malls and the mega stores (with floor area at about 8,000+ sq. ft.). The choice and the variety there are mindboggling. Therefore, on the food-front, there is absolutely nothing to worry about.

Local travel, sightseeing

Africa is a fabulously beautiful place, far from the artificial façade that you are likely to come across at many tourist spots worldwide. Grab the opportunities with both hands, travel as much as you can while you are there. See Mother Nature and the wildlife in all their glory. Do not be paranoid about saving your dollars. You may not get such opportunity again. Visit every nook and corner. Every place is different, and is worth visiting. The facilities are excellent and the whole region is geared towards making life enjoyable and entertaining for the tourists. Take advantage of that facility and travel.

Do not spend the weekends sitting at home. Most organizations, including the banks in many countries, have a five-day week. So that makes it convenient for weekend trips. Round up your friends, load the boot/trunk of your car with "bitings" (a typically local innovation meaning snacks) and soda (carbonated soft drinks) and take off on those trips. Of course, you'd have to drive yourself. You will find many destinations that are good for a two nights' stay at a reasonable distance from your home – say a three-to-four-hour drive, sometimes a bit longer. You can be out almost every weekend, like we were. Mark the relatively more distant places for visit when you have extended holidays (like the Easter). Apart from your ID cards and driving licence, don't forget to carry your binoculars and cameras with you (long lenses and a tripod are advisable). If you have a video camera, you will enjoy using it. Buy it right away, if you do not have one yet. In Africa, it is worth having these around.

Spotting the 'Big Five'

Among the most sought-after experiences for visitors to the African continent is spotting the Big Five. It's a term widely used in Africa by the game viewing tourists and safari tour operators. The term refers to the lion, leopard, rhinoceros, elephant, and African buffalo – being renowned for their size, strength, and the thrill they evoke when encountered on safari. It's an experience at the top of many travellers' must-do list.

The following are the places to visit when you are in Africa:

Maasai Mara National Reserve, Kenya. The visit there is an experience by itself. There are lots to see, hence keep some extra time in hand. Try to time your visit so that you can witness the Great Migration.

Amboseli National Park, Kenya. If you are travelling from Nairobi, it's near the Kenya-Tanzania border, on the way to Serengeti. Located at the foot of Mount Kilimanjaro across the border in Tanzania, the park is especially famous for its large herds of elephants. Lions, leopards, and buffaloes also roam the park's plains. Always worth a visit.

Serengeti National Park and Ngorongoro, Tanzania. It is actually a continuation of the Mara plains, but divided by the border of Kenya's neighbour, Tanzania. Ngorongoro is inside the very large crater of an extinct volcano, thickly populated by wild life.

Kruger National Park, South Africa. It is one of the largest game reserves in Africa, spanning nearly 20,000 sq. km. of diverse habitats. It is home to a significant population of all the Big Five species, including the endangered rhinoceros.

Chobe National Park, Botswana. It's renowned for its large herds of elephants, often seen congregating along the Chobe River. This pristine wilderness also supports thriving populations of lions, leopards, and buffaloes, completing the Big Five ensemble. Boat safaris are also available to see the wild life from a different perspective.

Hluhluwe-iMfolozi Park, South Africa. Located in South Africa's KwaZulu-Natal province, the park hosts all members of the Big Five and provides both guided safaris and self-drive opportunities.

This list is a poor representation of the unimaginable number of places – small and big, and the many wonders of Nature, that one should visit when in Africa.

A word of warning:

In some of the game reserves, including the privately owned ones, you may be allowed to explore the reserves on your own. That is, without a trained and experienced guide accompanying you. Be very careful when you do so. If you are accompanied by children, train them thoroughly to the following before you venture out.

Top of the list: Listen to your guide and obey his instructions to the letter. Do not force him or insist on doing things while on safari if he is reluctant or does not permit it. Disobedience could translate into risking your life.

Second: Never, never leave your vehicle, even for a second, while on safari. Disobeying this rule spells TROUBLE, yes big trouble.

Third: Never try to disturb the animals or try to draw their attention, say by offering food or throwing stuff at them. Heaven help you if they get upset or angry.

Fourth: Maintain total silence at all times. By 'total' I mean pin-drop silence. No excited chatter, no cross-talk, no stage whispers, no nothing at all. The maximum noise allowed may only be the click of the camera shutters, that's all.

Fifth: Always maintain a safe distance between your vehicle and the animals you come across. At too close proximity (*you* do not define what is 'too close', *the animals do*!) they may feel threatened and charge at you. You may have no idea at all how fast the rhinos can run. You will be surprised, but might be too late. Elephants are equally sensitive.

Sixth: Be responsible for the garbage you produce. Do not spoil the surroundings with your leftovers. Collect them and bring them back to your camp site for disposal.

Safaris

Safari camps and tour operators normally provide two trips a day – one very early in the morning, and another in the afternoon. Avail of them. These safaris will offer you plenty of opportunity to observe the big game and for photo shoots.

Night safari is also available at several camp sites. Take one, if you have time to spare. It's always worth it. You are sure to come across animals that hardly ever appear during the day.

More to come

Africa is a veritable wonderland for any visitor. The first sighting of wild elephants, large number of crocodiles basking in the along the Mara river, countless number of hippos jostling against one other in the water for space – will leave you spell bound. Zebra and deer roam about like herds of cattle. Hippos and crocs are too numerous to count. Initially, you may be too eager to capture them all in your camera before you move on.

But be patient. There are lots and lots like these to see. Your guide will know where the animals are, and will take you to the choicest of places, time permitting. Remember to tip them well when the safari is over.

Besides these game reserves of note, there are many other places of interest that you should visit if you are staying there for any length of time.

For example, you can enjoy the crystal clear water and the beach of white sands off Mombasa along the east coast of the continent, or the marine parks (including the one off the coast of Malindi) as you go snorkelling in the sea. Take a hot air balloon ride and watch the migration from the sky.

Victoria Falls, located on the border between Zambia and Zimbabwe, is one of the world's largest waterfalls, with a width of 1,708 m (5,604 ft.).

Another little known wonder is the Murchison Falls on the shore of Lake Albert, in northwest Uganda. It is the most powerful waterfall in the world. Every second, the equivalent of 200 bathtubs full of water is forced through a gorge less than seven paces wide.

Putting it in another way, at Murchison Falls, the Nile river squeezes through a gorge that is only 8m wide and plunges with a thunderous roar into the "Devil's

Cauldron" about 75 feet below, creating a trademark rainbow. The pressure of the water is so great that the ground trembles around it. And the noise that it makes round the clock can be heard from several miles away.

You can approach from the top where the Nile is still several hundred feet wide and flows calmly before being forced to squeeze into the gorge. Or take a cruise up the Paraa river right up to the gorge, and watch from a safe distance the fury and the cauldron. Both are unbelievable sights.

If you are in South Africa and have time to spare, take a train ride from Pretoria to Cape Town or back. It is a 54-hour journey of 600 kilometres (994 miles) by the Blue Train, through some of the most diverse and spectacular scenery offered by the African sub-continent. Alternately, Rovos Rail for many travellers offers the finest way to see the beautiful country of South Africa and its scenery on its journey between Cape Town and Pretoria.

Live life to the full. Need I say more?

CHAPTER X

Kolkata Mirror[7]

WILD, WILD EAST

(Travel tips by Rupnarayan Bose)

Posted On Friday, June 12, 2009 at 11:36:53 AM

[Continuing with the theme of tourism. This article was written at the request of and published by Kolkata Mirror. Now reprinted, slightly updated.]

For those who love to venture off the beaten track, a visit to any part of Africa can be an unforgettable experience. No amount of words is enough to do justice to the bounty that is on offer in this region.

------

[7] kolkata.mirror@gmail.com

The wide open space, the raw, natural beauty of the countryside, and the close encounter with wild life are guaranteed to make people wonder why they did not visit Africa much earlier.

Among the many must-see regions is East Africa, comprising Uganda, Kenya and Tanzania. Nairobi, the capital of Kenya, is the take off point for almost all tourists and visitors to East Africa. Nairobi is the largest and the most developed city in East Africa, the fourth-largest city in the whole of Africa, providing all modern amenities. There is a wide variety of restaurants, clubs, pubs, discos, movie halls, shopping malls, hypermarkets and casinos to choose from.

No amount of words is enough to do justice to the bounty that is on offer in this region. This story would remain incomplete if I did not mention the experience of having deep-fried Tilapia with chilled beer and Stony, while sitting on the lush green lawns of Jinja Sailing Club on the shores of Lake Victoria, with the cool breeze against my face, watching the Nile start its 3,000 km journey to the sea. You have to be there to know what I felt then!

Or visit the Bujagali Falls. Watch the roaring river Nile tumble over the rocks, as you enjoy your drinks and fries.

Choice of food

Thanks to about 100,000 strong population of Asian (read Indian) origin, Indian food is easily available and is of excellent quality. In Nairobi you can find superb quality food of every variety including Western style, Indian, Chinese, Japanese, Italian, French, Lebanese, Brazilian and local African cuisine. On safari, continental and western food are normally on offer, or suggest special dishes to the chef on duty. Incidentally, do not miss out dining at Carnivore or at Tamarind – just to name a couple of top quality restaurants there.

Means of travel

The main roads and highways are very well maintained. Driving at 175 km per hour on the Nairobi-Mombasa or along Nairobi-Thika highways for me was no big deal.

One drives on the left. Within the city and outside, you must give way to traffic from the right. If you wish to save time, pack in more in less time during your travel, or have funds to spare, short-haul flights by mainline or smaller aircraft from the JKIA or the Wilson Airport are easily available. A quick trip to Mara by plane instead of by road will not be a bad idea.

What to see

Start with Nairobi National Park, only eight miles from the city centre, bordering the highway from the airport to the city. It is famous in the whole world for being the only national park to be found within a capital city. It hosts over 100 animal species such as the rhino, lions, cheetahs (but no elephants) and an amazing 500-plus bird species.

The other places of interest within or close to the city are the National Museum, the Arboretum, Kenya Railway Museum, Kenya National Archives, giraffe centre at Langatta, Karen Blixen Museum and the Bomas of Kenya.

Just outside Nairobi

To the east and north-east, the Rift Valley, one of nature's great wonders, is an hour's drive from the city centre. A day trip can also be made to Lake Magadi to visit Olorgesailie in The Rift Valley for its prehistoric campsite.

Lake Naivasha also lies on the other side of Rift Valley, as does Maasai Mara. Nakuru National Park around Lake Nakuru and Lake Bogoria (home of hundreds of crocodiles and rhinos) are 155 km and 280 km away – good for a weekend trip. The thousands of pink flamingos at both these lakes is a sight to behold.

The dozens of hot springs at Lake Baringo will take your breath away; they are really alive, hot, and continuously shoot boiling water very high into the air ("very high" really means *very high*; you have stay far away if you don't want to get scalded).

Towards the north of Nairobi are Aberdare National Park (the home of rhinos, leopards and elephants), the Sweetwater Game Reserve, and the Mount Kenya National Park which provides a grand view of the highest peak in Kenya. Each of these destinations can be covered by way of a day-trip, but overnight stay is strongly recommended. Meru, Laikipia, Buffalo Springs, Samburu, Shaba are some of the other game reserves further north of Nairobi. Tsavo is to the south-east.

On the way to some of these places you may be fortunate to cross the Equator several times. The locations are well marked, with a prominently coloured line to show you the imaginary Equator. To prove the point, you may also be shown how a matchstick floating in a small bowl of water rotates in opposite directions when you take it across the Equator. Got to be seen to be believed.

This is also the country where, as the legendary hunter-naturalist Jim Corbett, who was invited to accompany the Royal party during their stay, wrote in the visitors' book:

> *"For the first time in the history of the world, a young girl climbed into a tree one day a Princess, and after having what she described as her most thrilling experience she climbed down from the tree next day a Queen – God bless her."*

The Maasai Mara

Usually referred to as 'The Mara', this is the place to visit, any time of the year. The place can be reached by road or by light aircraft. Mara Serena and Keekorok Lodges are the places to stay. Every tourist spot has high quality accommodation. The so-called "camps" are luxurious.

During your visit to Nairobi, if you are short of time, visit only Mara. It is a two-night, three-day trip – worth every penny of your long trip to Kenya. Four safaris (one daily in the early morning and another in the afternoon) are the norm on those trips. Balloon ride is available. Though it is as an experience of a life time, it comes at a price. If you are there when the migration takes place, make sure not to miss it. This could be the best opportunity to really make use of your video or still camera.

Stretch your visit a wee bit more. Visit Ngorongoro and Lake Manyara too. You will thank me later.

Incidentally, few talk about Botswana, the Okavango Delta region or Namibia. We might as well leave them for another day.

Safety and security

- While in the city stick to your group.

- Avoid walking out of your hotel unless it's within the immediate vicinity. Forget about your urge to explore. Stick to your hotel at all times. Taking a walk within most parts of the central business districts in Nairobi, is safe for locals (you are not) but only during the day time, and provided you do not carry valuables.

- Walking out alone at night is *not* recommended.

- Keep your valuables in a safe place. Do not wear, display or carry expensive items. Leave that Rado wrist watch or those gold bangles and chains at home in India. Use imitation jewellery, if you must. Do not tempt temptation.

- Limit the amount of cash carried to what you need only for cash purchases - most hotels, safari lodges and tour operators accept major credit cards. While going out for shopping go in a group, carry limited cash, and use transport recommended only by the hotel.

[There is no limit to how cautious you need to be. For example, when I went out of my office for lunch every day, I took off my wrist watch, my pen and wallet, and locked them up in my office drawer. I only carried a KES 500 note to pay for my lunch.]

- Kenya has three international airports (Jomo Kenyatta International Airport in Nairobi, Moi International Airport in Mombasa and Eldoret International Airport in Eldoret), four major domestic airports and over four hundred smaller aerodromes and airstrips.

Information about travel formalities, getting there, visa formalities, exchange rates and several photographs were printed with the originally published article, but deleted from this post since all information (and photographs) is nowadays easily available on the internet.

CHAPTER XI

THE ECONOMY

I am not an economist, nor an expert in economic matters. This is not a treatise or a research paper, but a thumb-nail profile of the situation (according to this author) obtaining at that time, and is obviously dated.

A number of countries in Africa are, in economic terms, a study in contrast. Some of them have no exchange control at all, and no restrictions whatsoever on the movement of capital across their borders. Others have, additionally, completely liberalized the banking sector, the financial services sector, as well as the insurance sector. Some of the African nations have already gone all the way. Everything has been privatized or freed of controls (in a few countries, with debatable consequences).

Some countries are, however, bureaucratic and more rigid than others. Some also continue to have balance of payment problems and, therefore, carefully control the flow of foreign exchange and the range of goods they import. Some welcome foreigners and foreign business initiatives, some don't. Some are just opening up to overseas investments.

In quite a few African countries, 'long term' means six months. Everything can be very fluid indeed, and therefore, uncertain. (Case to point: the economic downturn of Zimbabwe from 1999 t0 2009, or the resurgence of Uganda). It is difficult to make a five-year plan and stick to it. In some countries, even the bank fixed deposits (used to) offer only a maximum of six months' maturity, and no financial instrument whatsoever (including the Government's Treasury Bonds) is available for more than one year. Many countries have no stock exchanges yet.

For obvious reasons, it is not possible to delve into the economic backgrounds of these countries and other related issues in detail, neither is this the place to do so.

(This thumb nail picture is subject to updating based on current information.)

CHAPTER XII

A BANKER AT LARGE IN KENYA

I first set foot on African soil in early 1998 when I took charge (or so I thought) of a commercial bank of good reputation in East Africa as its MD and CEO. It was privately owned. Its chairman, who was also its major shareholder, was an industrialist – the second-largest plastic goods manufacturer in East Africa. He was a Kenyan citizen of Indian origin, a Gujarati whose parents had migrated to Kenya before he was born. There are about one hundred thousand people from the Indian sub-continent, commonly referred to as Asians, who had made Kenya their home and had contributed significantly to the economy of the region. In fact, the Gujaratis were the face of the entire business community in Kenya. (You may recall that the community was driven out of Uganda by Idi Amin, the economy of Uganda suffering heavily as a result. The government of Kenya was far wiser.) As is usual for Asian-owned banks, it had major exposure to the local Asian community in terms of its general business mix, particularly its lending portfolio. Owning a bank was matter of pride for the members of the Asian community Kenya. The bank in Kenya which I had joined, though small in size, was well-regarded.

The chairman was an entrepreneur at heart. He had built up his plastic business from scratch. He was similarly determined to build up his banking venture. He was very closely involved with both, and split his daily routine to make sure that he was involved in all the decisions taken at his factory as well as at his banking set up. As part of his routine, he held (hold your breath) two full-fledged Board meetings every week at the bank. Yes, these were Board meetings with all the trappings, including agenda items, minutes of past meetings, action taken reports and what have you. Present at these meetings were two of his local directors (partners in his plastic manufacturing company, but having no idea whatsoever about commercial banking), and the bank's "top management", i.e. my general manager and myself. At these meetings all papers and decisions taken by us were reviewed by him. Apart from the twice-a-week Board meetings, he also spent the first half of *every working day* at the bank – overseeing operations and meeting the bank's customers. The Central Bank of Kenya did not approve of his style of functioning, but one just couldn't keep him away from his bank.

My cabin was on the same floor. All the customers that visited us waved at me from outside my glass cabin, and walked on to the last cabin to meet the chairman. They knew where the real power lay, and who the dummy was. I often wondered what I was supposed to be doing there.

To go back a little, some of the rich Asians with money to burn had, years ago, set up finance companies for two-wheeler financing. The business model was simple, straightforward and needed no special expertise. But then, like all finance companies, they became unmanageable and the Central Bank of the country (Central Bank of Kenya or CBK) gradually became very worried with the way things were being handled at these finance companies. So, one day, these finance companies received letters from the CBK to the effect that they would have to convert themselves to commercial banks, and strictly follow from day one all the norms of a commercial bank. The Central Bank of Kenya (CBK) had decided that it was far easier to control and regulate a banking entity than a non-banking finance company (for which there were practically no way to regulate them)[8].

Some of these finance companies converted themselves into commercial banks, but continued to finance two-wheelers as they had done all along. It was their comfort zone. Others appointed professional bankers and tried to conduct banking business. I was the second MD and CEO to adorn this bank's chair, simply because the CBK wanted a

---

[8] In India, Dr. A. C. Shah Committee Report (1992) was the precursor to the tightening of the grip of the Reserve Bank of India (RBI) over the non-banking finance companies.

"professional" at the helm. In reality though, the chairman and the owner, who had created this institutions from the ground up, had no intention to loosen his grip over the bank or its operations. He did not trust external "professionals" to run *his* bank. Thus, the twice weekly Board meeting, and his half-day presence every day at the bank during the business hours. Most disconcerting for a banking professional who wanted to put in his best, as with Centurion bank at its inception.

The members of the Asian community gathered and exchanged notes quite frequently at many of the do's that one member or another organised over the weekends, all dressed up in their Sunday best. Such mid-day meets were called "jalebi-gathiya (ganthiya)" meets. It was a highly effective platform for networking.

To continue with our story, at one of these regular "Board meetings" the issue taken up for discussion was the penal rate of interest lately imposed by the bank on the defaulting borrowers. The chairman said that several of his customers (read, his friends and peers in the Asian community) had complained to him that the (penal) interest rates were too high; they hurt, and that the bank should do something about them. On behalf of the bank I explained that the penal rates were *meant* to be punitive – much higher than the normal rates. They were meant to act as deterrents or disincentives to potential defaulters, to keep their numbers as low as possible and thus improve the overall quality of the bank's loan portfolio. The main objective of a penal interest was *not* to increase the bank's income, but to impose financial discipline on the borrowers. The argument obviously did not go down well with the chairman.

He had another issue to dwell on. He said that some customers had to resort to frequent overdrawing of accounts, but were inconvenienced since they had to approach the bank every time they needed to draw beyond their sanctioned limits. He suggested that the bank should sanction 25 to 30 per cent over and beyond the quantum estimated after appraisal, in order to avoid frequent reporting to the Central Bank of Kenya, and inconvenience to his customers (not necessarily in that order!). While on the subject, he also made it known that he did not appreciate the bank (read, us) requesting the borrowers to visit the bank to execute loan documents. Why couldn't we, by way of "customer service", visit their offices instead, at *their* convenience, to execute security documents or loan applications? Could we also be extremely polite while writing letters to defaulters, non-performing borrowal account holders, or even while calling up bad loans, so that the bank did not hurt their sensibilities?

The issue uppermost in his mind was the fact that his peers were unhappy with him and his bank. They had complained to him at various social gatherings (probably in the presence of his other friends) that his bank was severely penalising them for occasionally stepping over the line, for frequent irregular drawings, or for failing to repay on schedule. The chairman strongly felt that such irregularities were normal to every business. A bank (especially a bank owned by a fellow Asian) was supposed to be 'understanding', rather than exploit these situations to inconvenience or penalise the borrowers to increase profit. As the owner of the bank, he was in a position to lend a helping hand, offer financial assistance, to the fellow members of his community; which he always did. However, by treating his peers as it had done, the bank was effectively undermining his position. In being strict, he felt that the bank was letting him down very badly indeed. That could not go on.

It was not very difficult to understand where he came from. His plastic manufacturing company enjoyed large financial facilities from other banks in Nairobi. As their customer, especially as a borrower, he knew exactly where the shoes pinched. Unfortunately, even as the chairman of the bank, he continued to wear the hat of a bank's customer/borrower. For him, the Chinese wall between his profession as an industrialist and as the owner of a bank did not exist. It was well-nigh impossible for him, therefore, to step into the shoes of a banker and to think like one. Neither would he trust us professionals to do so. Consequently, as the chairman of the bank he did not realise where his loyalty ought to lie.

Financial institutions of diverse descriptions operated in Kenya, Uganda and Tanzania. In Kenya, the insurance companies were allowed to be privately owned, as were banks. Highly reputed foreign banks from Europe, the USA and South Africa also occupied the banking space, as did a couple of banks of Indian origin.

By way of a footnote, let me add that the bank that I mention was taken over by a Nigerian conglomerate in 2013 and its original name was erased. It exists no more in its former avatar.

Interestingly, in spite of the upheavals including the change in ownership and management, the chairman landed on his feet. He continues to be the chairman of its operations in Kenya to this day.

[General observations:

- Since the lines often blurred, diversion of funds was common with some of the privately owned banks. The owners simply did not understand the gravity of the situation or the implications for the banks they owned. Frauds (sometimes by the owners themselves) and consequent collapse of banking institutions were therefore, not uncommon.
- When I resigned, the bank in my story above was a single branch operation and run on ethical lines. It now has 38 offices in the East African region.
- To bolster their operation the local banks often recruit experienced banker from banks like Bank of India, Bank of Baroda or foreign banks operating in the region.]

CHAPTER XIII

SPEAKING ABOUT SECURITY

This is the last but not the least of the issues that a visitor faces when travelling to Africa! On the contrary, this may head their lists of things to enquire about. Many people that I have met say that they have heard a lot about the security aspect, but know nothing about it specifically. Frankly, if you have not been there and haven't experienced it personally, you will never understand what I am talking about. I didn't, till I met fear face to face. Like the economic and political issues alluded to in the foregoing chapters, this also is a very delicate subject – for a variety of reasons.

I will just touch on a few areas of concern – especially those that are likely to affect a visitor, including looting of residential places, mugging, car-jacking and the like. (Highjacking of cars is 'popularly' known as car-jacking in most parts of Africa.)

My advice to you is to read between the lines. I'll leave the rest (including the gory details!) for discussions in person, if and when the occasion arises. Here goes:

i)   Carefully choose the place to stay. The approach to places including the entry point that is dark and lonely – especially at night – should be avoided.

ii)   If you join as a CEO or MD or a general manager, you may be entitled to a bungalow (an isolated, independent house) with a swimming pool and a football field sized lawn etc. thrown in for good measure. Although a boost for your ego and befitting your status, avoid such luxuries at all costs. Instead, opt for a well-protected apartment complex inside a gated community for you and your family. There is safety in numbers and in anonymity.

iii) Be very careful while stopping at the main gate while entering your residence. That's a point of extreme danger and a favourite target for car-jackers. It's because you or your driver would have to stop the car there and wait till the watchman or guard (askari) pushes open the gates wide enough for your car to drive in. If there are trees or bushes around the gate, or the place is not well-lit, it could be even more risky. Minimise the waiting period outside your entry point. Get inside as quickly as possible.

iv) At night, if you see a headlight behind you following you for long, do not try to go home or to enter your building complex directly. Drive straight on to the nearest police station.

v) Whether your office is in the central business district or in the suburbs, if you wish to step out of your office for a while, leave *all* valuables (your wallet, watch, rings, pen, etc.) in your desk drawer, lock it, and then go out with just enough money for your purchases or lunch.

vi)   Forget about taking a walk in the evenings. Such luxuries are not freely available everywhere. There are select places that are within protected compound walls and considered safe; stick to them for your constitutional. You will get to know about them soon after you arrive, so 'no sweat'.

vii)   While paying or receiving cash, do not display your wallet or how much money you carry therein. Do not display or count (your bundle of) cash in full public view. Do not tempt fate.

viii)   Working till late evening in your office is a habit that is best avoided. If you do, you may find yourself all alone in the central business district or around your office area, and an easy target for being mugged or car-jacked. Frequent departure from your office late at night will attract unwanted attention, hence beware.

ix)   When going out on week-ends, or (if you
        have to) for a late-night party/show, travel in
        a group. Get the last car to see you to the
        door or inside your housing complex.

x)   Travel together with several cars as a group
        when on a road trip. Driving all alone late at
        night is a strict no-no.

xi)   If you have a flat tyre at night – even within
        the city limits – do not stop to change it. Drive
        to the nearest petrol station, and only then
        carry out the repairs, or call a friend to pick
        you up. Get your car retrieved and repaired
        the next day.

xii)   If you face hijackers or car-jackers (close
        encounters of the unwanted kind) – do *not*
        hesitate, do not fumble, do not argue, do not
        try to act smart. It may cost you your life.
        Obey the hijackers' every instruction
        instantly, without question. Spending a bullet
        and taking a life are amazingly simple for
        them. So do not provoke, do not take
        chances and do not try to be a hero. Life is
        lot more precious than the money you may
        stand to lose.

xiii)   Do not keep the doors to your home open at any time of the day or night. Keep them securely locked at all times. Access should be allowed only after you are sure of the visitor's identity and intention. The gated communities have ID cards, gate passes and a system of calling in to confirm access. Cooperate with the gatekeepers. Inform them in advance if you are expecting friends.

xiv)   I can't say this enough, but always (always) maintain a low profile. Do not give any impression of being wealthy, having costly items or a significant amount of cash at home or on your person. Do not keep anything at home that you would regret losing.

xv)   Do not carry any item of value while on the road. Be prepared to be mugged at any time – even at mid-day, even around the central business district (CBD) of the city, in full public view.

xvi)   Do not carry anything in opaque envelopes to provoke undue interest and consequently, being mugged. Briefcases are out – for the same reason. If you are carrying documents outdoors, use a plastic cover, so that the contents are visible to anyone remotely interested.

xvii)   If you have a choice, get a car that stands out among the crowd, like being coloured different from the rest. Paint the number in very large fonts on your rooftop (so that the police can identify it easily from the helicopter above, if need be).

xviii) When you leave the car parked anywhere, do not leave anything of interest on the front or back seats, or anything clearly visible from outside that's so tempting as to provoke a break-in. If you have to leave any such item in the car, lock it up in the boot, away from prying eyes.

xix)   Keep your windows closed while travelling by car. Use the car air-conditioner, or keep the windows only a wee bit open at the top only for some fresh air. When you stop at traffic lights, be extra vigilant. Make sure that the glass window pane leaves only a small gap at the top (How small? I was advised that the gap should be wide enough to allow fresh air in, but keep the barrel of a gun out!). There, you have it! Quite simple.

xx)   Trust no one with your keys – especially your house or office keys. An impression can be made in an instant and the duplicate key used later. If you have to send a bunch of keys through a messenger or peon, for example, place the keys inside an envelope, close and seal it, sign on the face of the envelope so that it cannot be tampered with, and only then send them across. Make sure to enquire with the recipient that he or she has received the envelope or package unopened.

xxi)   Be very polite with your local house-staff, viz., driver, maid, sweeper or gardener. Do not give rise to any disagreement with them. Do not treat them badly. If you wish to terminate any of them, manoeuvre it in such a way that *they* are the ones to initiate the move to leave. Part as friends. Compensate them to their satisfaction. Do not for a moment think that you have lost in the bargain. Trust me, you haven't.

xxii)   Reverting to the subject of car-jacking, the administration department at the bank where I worked in Nairobi had circulated a note for our enlightenment. A copy of the same is reproduced verbatim later in this book. I am sure you will find it interesting, if not highly illuminating, to say the least.

The points about safety precautions might come as a culture-shock to many. For persons used to late nights on Brigade Road (Bangalore India), Park Street (Calcutta), Juhu-Chowpatty (or Marine Drive, Bombay), or The Marina (Chennai), the risk scenario brings home a very painful process of unlearning and re-learning, and a lot of getting used to. But ask anyone who has been to the big cities of any developed country viz. to Geneva, New York, Chicago, or the streets of L.A., and they will advise similar precautions there too. You may, therefore, term these only as a different shade of grey.

Once again, understand that all places do not carry the same degree of risk. Neither do people out there sit behind closed doors in fear at all times in spite of all that they may have experienced. They still go out and enjoy life. We did, in Kenya, Uganda and in Ethiopia.

The fact remains that dangers exist – sometimes at the most unexpected places. It is wise to be aware of it, and take steps *not* to invite trouble as far as possible. For whatever it is worth, you *have to* take precautions (it is called 'risk management'). I myself have seen many bank robberies happening in broad daylight, right in front of my eyes. Felt like a Western movie show in real life. I can now easily distinguish between a car backfiring and the sound of a rifle shot. Within 20 days of my first visit to Nairobi, the bank I headed was robbed at gun-point (six AK-47s and revolvers). Personally, I lost a considerable sum – as did the bank itself, as did the other members of staff (they too were stripped of all their valuables). I am extremely lucky to be alive today (the gun was an inch from my chest, and the guy was very eager to pull the trigger). It took me more than two whole years and more to get over the shock and the trauma, that too only partly.

The lesson? Enjoy the best that Africa has to offer. At the same time, be prepared, so that you avoid the risks or occupational hazards that may exist in some of the countries there. The precaution will save you many a tear.

For those intending to do business with Africa, a bit of unsolicited advice. Do not go by your experience in India, or with other countries. Each place, each country, in Africa as elsewhere, is different. For example, the Nigerian scams[9] are unique stories by themselves, I'll leave them for another day. Yet, goods are being exported to Nigeria, business is being done by the rest of the world with Nigeria. Ethiopia as a country is quite different from Zimbabwe or Rwanda or Congo or Tanzania.

The situation is rarely static, changing with the times. Years later I spent two months in Ethiopia. I enjoyed my stay there, faced no risk at all. Yes, during my short stay, I witnessed a single instance of mugging of a colleague of mine that happened right around the corner from the place where I lived, but that's all there was.

Therefore, research your destination and your customer(s) fully, and then chart your course. Ask

---

[9] Have to be described – from the visiting exporter's point of view.

those who had been to your probable destination in Africa, had done business there. Seek information from the Net, your High Commissioner stationed there, and take all the necessary precautions as dictated by the feedback received and your common sense. Going in blindly (even if it's for a personal, fact-finding trip), or without proper research, is never advisable.

CHAPTER XIV

HOW TO SURVIVE A CAR-JACKING

[There were no WhatsApp those days, nor the all-pervasive social media that we nowadays take for granted. While working in Kenya, I received the following in the form of a copy on an A-4 sized paper, unsigned, that was in circulation. I reproduce below its content verbatim, warts and all. Author unknown. RB.]

In the last two weeks (says the note, received by me sometimes in the year 1999 - RB) there have been according to press reports a weekly average of 10 cases of car-jacking in Nairobi alone. There are probably more that are not reported, not to mention what happens in the other parts of the country.

From my experience I feel it is fair to bring to your attention some observations which will definitely reduce your chances of being involved in such a traumatic experience.

1.   Anybody can become a victim and this is the first one as to realize. Living in an upmarket well-guarded suburb can give one a false sense of security as car-jackers have been known to strike anywhere and they do it at lightning speed.

2.   Virtually all car-jacking in Nairobi take place between 1800 and 2100 hours. (I beg to differ. In my experience the relatively safe hours are between 0400 and 0700 when the traffic is light, consequently the opportunities are few – RB.) Majority of those that take place outside these times have other targets as well e.g. prior knowledge of large amounts of cash. There is need to be extra careful during these times and month-ends are peak business times for car-jackers.

3. Vehicles that are particularly prone are white saloons (would you like to know why? – RB) especially those of Japanese origin (puchho 'kyun?' – RB). Station wagons (4X4) are also in fairly high demand for cross-border trade.

4. Areas that are most prone to car-jacking are stop-junctions, traffic lights, petrol stations, ATM centres, homes, offices and drop off/pick up points for your spouse/children. (That leaves out what? - RB) Avoid topping up tanks in the evenings or visiting ATMs if possible and be extra careful when you have to stop; e.g. the way one positions the car matters a lot. Be very sensitive as you approach a place where you have to stop e.g. by looking out for strangers loitering outside your compound, apparently neglected handcarts (mkokotenis), people who are not crossing the road when they should do so at lights – you will be surprised how much you notice when are watchful. When you stop keep the vehicle in first gear in case you have to take off fast – they rarely shoot at a vehicle once it has left.

5.   With the introduction of car-track a new breed
      of car-jackers has come up whose aim is not
      really the car but to drive you with your ATM
      card and force you to withdraw as much as it
      will allow. Do not carry your ATM card around
      with you at night if you can avoid it.

6.   Stationery vehicles are a magnet to car-
      jackers, so do not stop unnecessarily and
      always try to stop in well–lit centres.

7.   Avoid all major highways at night, if you do not
      come across car-jackers, most probably the
      spike-planting thugs (they plant a mat with
      sharp spikes or nails on the roads to induce
      punctures, and then pounce – RB) will get you.

8.   Avoid regular and predictable schedules in
      your movements – not very easy but it helps.

9.   Have your vehicle serviced regularly – look at
      the service tag and stick to the schedules. You
      will have less chance of breakdowns and your
      vehicle will always give you optimum
      performance. Before driving off especially in
      the evening inspect your off-side tyres. A slow
      puncture can develop into a flat in the middle

of nowhere, which makes you a lot more vulnerable to car-jacking.

10. If possible, travel with your dog(s) – they are a deterrent. Vehicles with more than two passengers are also less vulnerable.

11. In the event that all precautions fail and you happen to be accosted by the car-jackers, please

   a) Do not show any sign of resistance.

   b) Do not act out of impulse – this requires a considerable amount of rehearsal; i.e., for gentlemen not to impulsively try to hit back, or for ladies not to scream! All car-jackings in this country involve firearms and you will not have much chance to scrutinize whether it is a genuine firearm or a toy. (The author of this note was not trying to be funny – believe me. Further, you are advised not to stare at their faces or try to memorise how they look. They might kill you instead if you try to do that. They are not looking for recognition or want to be recognised. – RB)

c)   Follow their instructions and cooperate with them. They rarely want to kill but have no qualms at all about doing so if they meet with the slightest resistance. It's just another bullet! (So, be extremely polite, do not get provoked. Surrender, and instantly comply with every command with abject humility if you want to stay alive – RB). They will always want to drive you to a location far enough to give them adequate time to get away.

d)   After all this, you may require a bit of psychological counselling, otherwise you could remain shaken for months and end up being a very unsafe driver. (So true. Ask me, I have been there! – RB)

I COULD HAVE DIED THAT DAY

Within 20 days of my arrival in Nairobi, Kenya, I was less than a second away from being shot dead, point blank. This is the personal account of that horrific moment that I can never forget.

It was my first ever visit to Nairobi and East Africa. Till the job was offered to me at the end of the second day's interview, I did not know in which part of the globe Kenya was, or how its capital city of Nairobi was for a longish stay. I came home from the interview and traced Nairobi with the help of my son's school Atlas. Internet revealed precious little information except the fact that the city was situated at an altitude of 5,500 feet, almost on the Equator, and that the highway from the airport to the city proper actually passed through Nairobi National Park. One could see animals roaming around as one drove along the motorway.

The year was 1998, and the period was the first week of March when I joined my new assignment in a completely new city, in a new country/continent. Thankfully I was joining a commercial bank, a business that I happened to know well. The weather was brilliant, the sky as blue as one could ever find at 5,500 feet above the sea level. The temperature rarely strayed beyond 22 degrees C, I was told. Modern, tall buildings dotted the cityscape. I felt great. I formally joined the bank the next day.

Not more than 20 days had passed since my arrival in Nairobi, Kenya, when my world turned upside down. Of course, during the course of those 20 days I had been initiated in to some of the security aspects (euphemism for the lack of security, actually) prevailing in the city. For example, one day when I was about to leave office with some papers in a brown envelope my secretary suggested that I carry them in a plastic folder instead ('people' would know that I was carrying only documents, not valuables).

Another day when I was about to leave for lunch, I was advised to take off all valuables on my person and leave them in my office drawer, lock it, and just carry the minimum cash required to pay for lunch. Mugging was common, they said; particularly so when people see you coming out of a bank. So I took off my wrist watch, my pen, the ring on my finger, and left them along with the wallet before I stepped out of the building.

The fancy brief case I purchased in Bombay just prior to my flight to Nairobi was also a strict 'no-no'. It could be snatched very easily. If left on the seat of my car, it would be visible, and serve as an open invitation to a break-in and theft. For, a briefcase conveyed the intention to keep (valuable) articles inside, out of sight. So, no brief case, no opaque carry case and no item of value on your person, please. The simple message was: carry nothing that you do not wish to lose. Incidentally, imitation jewellery was all that the ladies there wore, fashion be damned. (I learned a lot more as days went by.)

The unlearning and re-learning process was a torture for someone like me. Many a times I had enjoyed sitting on the promenade at Bombay's Worli Sea Face at 1.30 am in the morning, not a soul in sight, totally at peace with the world, watching the white foam and hearing the sounds of the crashing waves, the sea breeze blowing against one's face. I relished the solitude but suffered no apprehension. Carrying a briefcase with substantial sums in it was common in Bombay or Bangalore. From Bombay to Nairobi, therefore, was quite a culture shock. For the uninitiated, it does take a while to get used to the security concerns one had to contend with. It was still far Too early for me to make the habits a part of my routine when the real thing actually hit me – brutally, with full force – within 20 days of my landing in Kenya.

It was 2.10 p.m. and the lunch hour was on. Several of the bank's staff had gone home for lunch. The office was nearly empty. I had finished the sandwiches I had brought with me to the office (my wife was yet to join me from India) and had left my chair to visit the wash-room. As I got out of my cabin I came face to face with a tall African man (another was right behind the first), carrying guns. The one near me asked if I was the senior most in the bank. I said that I was and asked if I could help him. I did not notice my staff signalling me frantically from behind the two gentlemen.

"Then you *do have* the keys to the vault", insisted the man.

I said that I did not, that it was with the head cashier who had gone home for lunch. "No, you are lying. You are the senior most; you hold the keys," insisted the man with the gun. He gave me a rough push towards the vault. I was not used to such behaviour and protested immediately. Again, I noticed the frantic gestures of one of my staff, but didn't catch the meaning.

The man said something in Swahili which I failed to understand. Seeing the blank look on my face the guy switched to English. He said, "No, you are the senior most. We know you have the keys to the vault. Give me or I shoot". Once again, he gave me a rough push with the gun towards the vault.

It took quite a while for the penny to drop. With total disbelief it dawned on me that my bank was actually being raided by dacoits, that the gun pointed at my chest was real, it was an AK-47 meant for robbery and not for protection, that the men were live dacoits. They meant business, were serious about their demands and also were in a hurry. As a few other staff members and I were herded towards the vault, I tried to put it across to them that I really did not have the keys, that I was the managing director and MDs did not hold cash or vault keys, that the cashiers held them.

By that time we were inside the vault. I did not know from where they had received their information, but they insisted that I must be having the keys, and that if I did not give them the keys they'd shoot. The AK-47 pointed straight at me, the business end of the barrel touching my chest. One of the girls started to weep (out of fear or apprehending my impending demise, I did not know). Another joined her. I did not know what to do or how best to react to the situation. If I did not have the keys, how could I produce them anyway, even if it was to save my own life! Once again I tried to tell them that the key was not with me.

Time was getting on. Seconds ticked by. They were getting delayed. The dacoits normally do not take more than five minutes to finish their act and be on their way in their getaway vehicle. And here they were, facing an obstinate banker. They got fed up, got anxious about the delay, and said 'fine, no keys, we shoot' and again pushed the gun against my chest, ready to pull the trigger and make his point.

From all the horror stories I had heard during the past 20 days, I knew that killing came to the dacoits and car-jackers as a matter of routine. I realised that this was it. Let me tell you that no one who has not faced such a situation would ever realise what it feels to be seconds away from certain death. Nothing, but nothing, can describe that feeling. For a fleeting moment I wondered if the pain would last more than a few seconds. I said a quick good bye to my worldly relations, and steeled myself for the bullet that was sure to follow. I felt a strange emptiness within me. Time stood still. This was *it*. So, this was how it ended. It was a matter of seconds now.

Just then, one of the members of staff chimed in from behind, "Sir, I have the keys". He produced a set of keys from somewhere, gave them to the dacoits, and guided them to the cash 'vault'. A couple of robbers busied themselves emptying the safe of cash. Others ordered us in Swahili to lie face down on the floor of the vault room. The command being in Swahili, it failed to register. Someone translated it in English for my benefit. But the robbers had no time for such niceties. One of them gave me a mighty push and I was face down flat on the floor in my suit and tie. Everyone was similarly ordered to lie down and not move an inch.

The 'vault' (actually it was the hand safe) was cleaned out. As I lay flat on the floor, one of the robbers noticed my raised hip pocket and took out the wallet. It had all the money that I had carried from India (about $1,100). It also had my driving licence and my Rotary club ID card. The wallet was taken. The diamond ring was snatched from my finger. Others were similarly robbed of their belongings.

I learned later that a few of the gang members with guns were watching over some of the other staff in another wing of the office. They were also robbed of their belongings. All the while the robbers were in continuous touch on their walky-talkies with their counterparts somewhere outside. (Later one of my staff told me that they were continuously being informed if any alarm had been sounded from our office or not. Our office was connected by an alarm system with the local police station. The attack had been sudden. The alarm had not been activated.) Before departing, they warned that they were leaving a guard behind to watch us. None of us was to get up or alert anyone. Then the office went absolutely quiet.

The girls kept on weeping as softly as possible. Silence continued to prevail. None dared to move.

After quite some time – no idea how long – someone murmured that the dacoits had probably gone. We turned our heads sideways very carefully, peeped through our half-closed eyes, shifted our hands and feet, felt no resistance or the prodding of guns, and slowly stood up. Then it was total chaos.

The cries and the weeping got louder. Voices were raised, people started talking all at once. Everyone had some story to tell. Someone informed the police. Another informed the chairman. We tried to assess the damage.

There were personal losses. Fortunately, no one had been hurt. More fortunately, the main vault was still untouched. In banks, a common practice is to keep the operating cash in a steel safe called the 'hand safe'. This safe, located near the vault room, is used during the day for frequent operations. Excess cash from the cash counters is stored in the 'hand safe', shortfalls were met from it too. However, the bulk of the stock of cash is always kept in the vault, in a reinforced concrete room protected by massive steel doors. It is opened once in the morning and once at the close of the day (unless a major demand or supply situation arises, or cash remittance is effected).

Possibly because the dacoits were getting late, or because they did not know the difference between a hand safe and a cash vault (which I doubt), or both, they had left with the money they looted from the hand safe. The major stock had been left untouched.

Losses suffered by the staff and the bank were compensated later by the insurance company. Realising that I would be 'upset', one of the directors took me out for dinner in a lovely Italian restaurant which had a live band playing golden oldies. I went home very late at night. The after-effects hit me only the next day. At office someone came to me with a few words of platitude, saying that such things were routine there. 'It is Africa... after all.....you know....such things happen!' I erupted, and told him that he did not know what he was talking about. I pushed him out of the cabin, locked the door. Then the dam burst. I cried my heart out for the next 60 minutes, till I had no more tears left. My secretary understood. She kept everyone away till I opened my cabin door once again.

I remained in shock for a long time thereafter. I almost made up my mind to leave Africa. (I had heard that a few days earlier three software professionals from a reputed company in India had been mugged in broad day light in the city centre. They had caught the flight back home the same evening.) It took all the persuasive powers of the chairman and some of the board members to keep me back in East Africa. However, for the next 12 months I virtually stopped stepping out of my office building, using the basement car park for all arrivals and departures. If I happened to suddenly brush against any local person while walking along the pavement, a chill used to run down my spine. Perspiration used to break out all over me, my entire being gearing up for another round of terror. The experience at the bank had left a deep scar in my psyche. For the first time in my life, I learned the real meaning of fear.

Something strange happened two months after this traumatic incident. Through ordinary mail, a badly addressed envelope sporting a ten-shilling stamp arrived on my table. I was puzzled, since I was new in Africa and expected no letter from any local source. I wondered who could have sent it, and cautiously opened the envelope.

Inside, I found my driving licence and the Rotary Club ID card that had been in the wallet taken away by the bank robbers. They were kind enough to return these to me, that too at their own expense.

Hakuna matata.

(Disclaimer: Every word of the above narrative is true.)

CHAPTER XVI

WHY AFRICA?

(An expat's point of view.)

Well, why not, may I ask?

I cannot blame you if you are wondering by now, if the situation is *that* worrisome on several fronts, why (the *&%#*) go there at all! But people do, not from India alone, but also from the developed world. Many Americans, British and Europeans came to Africa with certain objectives, not for a long stay initially, but they never went back. They made Africa their home. Not all of them were crazy.

Let's look at the brighter side of things for a change.

a) Career-wise, you might get a break that you will not get in the normal course at your home state.

b) The main reasons to relocate is the jump you are offered in terms of career and compensation packages, including much higher income and the savings potential. What you earn in India or in the UK in three years, in Africa you may earn in one (or less).

c) As I said earlier, if you are fortunate to earn in Africa and spend in low-cost countries like India, you save much more than if your family happens to be stationed with you in Africa.

d) The life-style is something one can hardly scoff at. (I used to go for my weekly vegetable shopping, or to the local supermarket for provisions, driving my own Mercedes car which, as an officer of the State Bank group in India, I could never have dreamed of doing in my life-time.)

e) The saying goes that (there is) 'No hurry, no worry in Africa'. Make no mistake – the people there are very hard working. Yet, life is as tough in the developed countries as it is comfortable in Africa. Those working in the developed countries like U.K., Canada, Europe or the U.S. have to put in hours of very hard work throughout the week, and then spend the week-end catching up with their personal work. Living space is far more spacious in African estates, even if you are not among the Richie-rich.

f) In contrast, as an expatriate what you'd enjoy in Africa would be luxury on all fronts elsewhere, especially if you can land an executive position, and know what to negotiate for. Apart from a good salary and spacious accommodation (most upscale residential complexes include swimming pool, jogging track and gym), count in the imported cars, club membership, golf on week-ends, and parties or get-togethers every other day. The working hours are not killing either – usually from 8.0 a.m. to 5.30 p.m. (five-day week), if you are not the kind who is in the habit of staying late at office every day. If you were inclined to stay late, you'd be advised to leave in good time before the locality becomes lonely, quiet and hence, risky.

g) Plenty of time to spare during the weekdays – for visiting friends, shopping, or dining out. The weekends are always more exciting, if you plan in advance.

h) You get to meet and know very closely a large number of very nice people, many of whom will remain your friends for time to come.

i) For senior and top executive expatriates, the salary or the life-style is indeed one that can hardly be experienced back home (Yes, by 'home' I *do* include not only India, but the advanced countries too.) The same can be said about the middle level executives as well. These, plus the benefit of experiencing a great continent in all its beauty that can be seen nowhere in the rest of the world, is a heady combination that few have been able to resist. Africa is, actually speaking, a continent that offers you the best of both worlds.

j) I have touched on this aspect earlier. Believe me when I say that I know of scores of people who have migrated to US, Canada, UK and other dream destinations and, upon arrival, bitterly regretted their decision to leave Africa. Their regret was deep indeed, and remained so especially during the initial years – till some of them made good, adjusting and settling down to their new environment abroad. Others had to make do with simply surviving somehow, while continuing to crave for the life they'd left behind home. Given a chance, they would have loved to get back – any day!

Reason enough to take the plunge? If I hear you say 'Yes', I will be the first one to agree with you (in spite of my encounter with the AK-47!).

CHAPTER XVII

WHAT'S SO INTERESTING ABOUT AFRICA, ANYWAY? [10]

Africa is a continent south of Europe, between the Atlantic Ocean and the Indian Ocean.

Countries in Africa:

Algeria, Angola, Benin, Botswana, Burkina Faso, Burundi, Cameroon, Central African Republic, Chad, Comoros Islands, Democratic Republic of the Congo, Djibouti, Egypt, Equatorial Guinea, Eritrea, eSwatini (formerly Swaziland), Ethiopia, Gabon,

---

[10] Source: http://www.interesting-africa-facts.com/

Gambia, Ghana, Guinea, Guinea-Bissau, Ivory Coast, Kenya, Lesotho, Liberia, Libya, Madagascar, Malawi, Mali, Mauritania, Morocco, Mozambique, Namibia, Niger, Nigeria, Republic of the Congo, Rwanda, Sao Tome and Principe, Senegal, Sierra Leone, Somalia, South Africa, South Sudan, Sudan, Tanzania, Togo, Tunisia, Uganda, Western Sahara, Zambia, Zimbabwe.

People of Africa

- Africa is said to be the cradle of mankind. This where it all began. The oldest human remains ever discovered were found in Ethiopia. They are approximately 200,000 years old. The earliest pre-human fossils were found in Kenya, Tanzania and South Africa.

- The African continent has the second largest population in the world, at about one billion people.

- Well over one thousand languages are spoken by the people of Africa. Some estimates put this number closer to two thousand.

- The largest religion in Africa is Islam, followed by Christianity.

- The African population is approximately 14.72% of the world's population (as of 2009).

- In my humble opinion, after visiting the wild life, the natural wonders like the hot springs or the Great Rift Valley of East Africa, no other place in the world will be able to satisfy your wanderlust.

Africa Landforms

- The longest river in the world, the Nile (4,132 miles), is located in Africa.

- Major rivers include the Congo, the Nile (the longest river in the world), the Zambezi (including the Victorian Falls), the Niger, the Ubangi and the Orange.

- The geography includes deserts, rain forest jungles, mountains, grasslands, hot springs, falls, rivers and lakes.

- Africa has the world's largest desert, the Sahara, which is almost the size of the United States. The Kalahari is another.

- Victoria Falls is the largest waterfall in Africa; it is 355 feet high and one mile wide.

- Mount Kilimanjaro is the highest mountain on the continent. It towers over 19,300 feet, which is so tall that glaciers can be found at its summit even though the mountain is near the equator.

- Madagascar is the largest island in Africa and the fourth largest island in the world. It is in the Indian Ocean off the East coast of Africa.

The continent

- Africa is the second largest continent on earth, approximately 11.7 million square miles.

- Africa straddles the equator and is the only continent to extend from the northern temperate zone to the southern temperate zone.

[If you think that the Equator is only an *imaginary* line on the map, then try out this experiment:

Take a bowl of water. Place a matchstick carefully on the surface of the water so that it floats. Swirl the water a little bit to make the matchstick naturally circle around the bowl. Now gently move the bowl of water across the Equator – that 'imaginary' line – and watch the matchstick's circular motion reverse and change direction – from clock-wise to anti-clock wise or vice versa! Try it out any number of times. You'll get the same result. The line *does* exist! – RB]

- Africa is the hottest continent on earth.

- Africa is where human beings first appeared on earth and the home of the world's first great civilization, Egypt, which dates back to 3300 BC.

- Sudan was Africa's largest country (968,000 square miles), before it was broken up into two.

- Africa covers 6 percent of the earth's total surface and 20.4 percent of the total land area.

- Cairo is the continent's largest city.

- Long before humans were around (the early Mesozoic Era) Africa was joined to the other continents in a massive continent called Pangaea. Over millions of years this huge continent broke apart shaping the world landscape as we know it today.

- India was a part of this continent before it tore away, creating the Great Rift Valley during the process. Indian land mass drifted across what is now known as the Indian Ocean, collided against the Asian land mass and formed the Himalayas.

- The East African Rift Valley, which divides the Somalian and Nubian tectonic plates, is the location of several important discoveries of human ancestors by anthropologists. The active spreading rift valley is thought to be the heartland of humanity, where much human evolution likely took place millions of years ago. (It is likely to tear apart from the mainland once again. Watch this space! ☺)

Animals

- Animal life in Africa is extremely diverse and includes lions, elephants, giraffes, hippopotamuses, gorillas, chimpanzees, zebras, rhinoceroses, crocodiles, leopards, cheetahs and birds like flamingos, herons, pelicans and storks.

- In Africa, the Big Five game animals are the lion, leopard, black rhinoceros, African bush elephant, and the African buffalo.

- The world's largest land animal is the African elephant.

- The world's tallest animal, the giraffe, lives in Africa.

- The fastest land animal in the world, the cheetah, lives in Africa.

- Africa is home to the world's largest reptile, the Nile crocodile.

- The gorilla, which can be found in the continent's jungles, is the world's largest primate.

To summarise, Africa is where you will meet a very fine set of people wherever you happen to be, and Mother Nature in all her unparalleled beauty.

The final point: The quality of life that you would enjoy in Africa promises to be far better than what you are likely to enjoy anywhere else. (OK, shoot me, but that's my opinion for now!)

CHAPTER XVIII

ETHIOPIA AT A GLANCE

[I mention Ethiopia, because I was there for a very short while, more like a whistle-stop tour. Written after a short stay of just two months (June-July 2014) in Addis Ababa, this is (was) my impression of Ethiopia in brief. I spent almost every working day in office. Went on a sight-seeing trip only once (organised tourism does not exist, nor tourism as an industry.). Hence, this is not an in-depth study of Ethiopia or an expert comment, but only an overview from a very limited perspective, shared for whatever it is worth. E&OE – as the say. You are sure to find more up-to-date information from many other sources, including the Net.]

++++

- Vast land area, lakes, mountains. No animals, no wildlife. (The locals tell us jokingly that all animals have migrated to Kenya.)

- Ethiopia introduced its first ever railways service shortly after we left Ethiopia in 2014. The construction of the railway system was nearing completion when we were about to leave Ethiopia.

- There is no tourism industry to speak of here, and no regular inflow of tourists. Unlike its neighbour Kenya, the tourism infrastructure in Ethiopia is at a very nascent stage even now. However, Addis has a rich night life.

- Driving around Addis at any time of the day or early evening is perfectly safe. Of course, it is never wise to invite trouble by being at lonely, dark places at odd hours of the night.

- Sightseeing: The access to far-flung places is difficult, the roads are not always good. The highways are, of course. Many of the places of note are at least one to two days' journey away. It's very costly, too. On arrival, you are likely to feel let down, disappointed with what you find (that's what we had been told, yet to experience it ourselves).

♦ Photography: Pictures taken using mobile phone is OK, perhaps. Perhaps it still does not look like a threat. But if you take out your long-lens DSLR camera in public, you better be very, very careful. The locals are very allergic to being photographed. They will refuse vehemently if you point your camera lens at them. Some may even demand money for being photographed. The allergic reaction to cameras could be a cultural problem (I am not sure), so be kind and respectful. Anyway, it is always advisable to seek permission before photographing a person.

♦ If you are an avid photographer, you may regret not being able to shoot to your heart's content, because of the many restrictions there. It's also because the Ethiopian men and womenfolk are probably some of most attractive looking and beautiful in Africa, if not the world.

♦ You are not allowed to photograph government buildings. Practically every other building being government owned, your options within the city are limited. Do be careful where you point your mobile camera or your telephoto lens. The advice of your auto or car driver could come in handy.

- Dairy products are generally in short supply.

- The country has no direct access to the sea. All its export and import are through Djibouti.

- High quality cinema houses present the latest movies.

- Western and Indian style restaurants are aplenty. You are likely to be spoilt for choice. Prices are reasonable too.

- Salt is hardly ever used. Carry a salt dispenser with you when invited to partake of Ethiopian food.

- Some dishes are terribly spicy. Hence, choose your dishes carefully.

- I enjoyed some excellent salad dishes while in Addis. Cannot forget their taste, even to this day.

- Being a vegetarian or vegan or veggie does not mean what it is supposed to mean to you and me. A vegetarian dish could include fish, egg or any other 'non-veg' item. You would have to make sure what you are being served with when you order a 'vegetarian' dish (say, a veg pizza).

- Mutton does not necessarily mean goat meat. It could be beef or anything else, just like 'mutton' in China means dog meat.

- People here (still) eat raw meat. Raw meat is served at parties alongside cooked food. You may have trouble distinguishing between the two, if you do not ask.

- Coffee: Ethiopian coffee is famous all over the world. The coffee that is usually served here is strong and dark – no milk, a bitter brew. Try machhiato. You will be served a tiny cup containing an extremely strong, dark brew with no milk or sugar added. I tried it once; couldn't finish it in spite of my best efforts, even though I love coffee. Not to be intimated, I carried a few packets of coffee when I left Addis for home.

- The gap between the rich and the poor is very wide. There is no middle class. Nobody rides a two-wheeler; you will not see any on the road. People stand in mile-long queues, travel by bus, mini buses and taxis or walk long distances. The rich travel by car (if at all they live in Ethiopia!).

♦ I was told that foreign funds were coming in, huge investments were being made. The signs were all there.

♦ "There is no risk here", they'll tell you. But why invite trouble? So don't carry valuables with you outdoors. (My colleague was mugged right on the lane leading to our building complex. Could be an exception.) Massive, strong gates, surrounded by high walls topped with barbed wire – some of them electrified – is a common sight. Watchmen and metal detectors are everywhere. But people move around freely during the day and the evening hours. Unlike some of the other cities, it's quite safe around these parts particularly during the day or early evening.

♦ Ethiopia is supposed to have surplus power. Yet, the supply is erratic, power cut is frequent and prolonged. (Someone say sarcastically that the country is depriving its citizens to earn from sale across the borders.)

- Left hand side drive. Horns are rare. Traffic from left has priority. Traffic jams are common.

- They follow the Julian calendar, not the Gregorian calendar. All months have 30 days. So, they have a much shorter thirteenth month (30 days x 12 months+ five days=365). Consequently, they have no leap year. Their festival days (like the Easter, or the New Year) are also different from the English calendar.

- Be careful about how you keep track of local time. According to local custom, four o'clock means 10 am. Our 8 pm is their 2 o'clock. Their days start from 6 am. Their clock is reset every 12 hours. Be careful while setting up an appointment with your girlfriend in Addis Ababa! But it is not an issue for visitors, really. Everyone is used to the 24-hour, 60-minute time keeping system that we are used to.

- Many of the locals do not bathe every day. They believe that doing so would harm their skin.

- The power outlets here have two pins. Plugs points at most places have no switches. Very few plug outlets in a room, absolutely minimalistic in this respect.

♦ Dictatorship style of governance. Almost every enterprise belongs to the government.

♦ High-cost society. Items cost as much as INR X 3.

♦ Too many underage/child beggars on the streets.

♦ This country has no foreign bank. Even though every other bank has the word 'international' as part of its name, none has any office outside Ethiopia, nor is global in its operation. 'Frog in the well' approach, may be.

♦ Ethiopia was never under any colonial rule, ever. The only one of the two countries in the entire continent of Africa to be so. The Ethiopians are fiercely proud about it for justifiable reasons.

CHAPTER XIX

HOME TRUTHS ABOUT FOREIGN POSTINGS[11]

(To make an overseas assignment work, employers need more than an eager executive with a suitcase. They must also motivate the staffer's spouse. Thus says a recently published Business Week survey.)

In this era of globalization, large number of employees are sent abroad by their companies every year. Corporations make big investments,

---

[11] I have included it with the hope that it may be useful to those planning a move to Africa or a new destination abroad in future. Source: https://www.bloomberg.com/news/articles/2002-07-14/home-truths-about-foreign-postings.

which can cost to or three times what it would to employ the same exec. Locally.

A new report corroborates growing evidence that keeping an expat's spouse happy is a good way to start making these assignments a success. One of the key findings of the report is that spouses who have been prepared for the move tend to be happier than those who haven't been familiarised with the culture of their destination. For example, some 30.5% of the 194 women surveyed were offered language training before their departure – and those people adjusted much better to their host culture than those with no prior language classes.

ASK FIRST: The subjects had relocated to countries such as France, Spain, Israel, Jordan, Thailand, China, Mexico, Britain, and Russia. A mere 6.2% of these women were consulted about the move by their spouse's employer before the decision was made and it is these women who were better able to deal with the experience than the majority, who had no consultation.

TROUBLES ADJUSTING: According to another report, 92% of expatriates blamed assignment failures on partner dissatisfaction, and 90% said they were caused by family concerns. A botched assignment risks a company's investment in an otherwise valuable employee.

KEEPING CONNECTED: Spouses adjust better when their husbands were readily available to attend such events as children's birthdays or school functions, the study found. Spouses who join local social networks also adjust better to their new lives. Moreover, spouses who were able to continue in their chosen pursuits while abroad – be it a job, a hobby, or volunteer work – embraced the international assignments far better than those who could not.

QUALITY TIME: What can the HR managers do to help execs improve the chances that an assignment will be successful? While foreign assignments can be demanding, companies need to make a point of setting aside time for their execs to be with their families, the report says. And, the study says, finding ways to help spouses hold onto their professions is important – including identifying career enhancing volunteer work or training programmes.

[Wise words, these. So before you decide to relocate, look into these aspects too, if you wish to make a success of your career abroad.]

Two decades later, an 'update':

THE TIMES OF INDIA

(Mar 21, 2022)

OVERSEAS DESI EXECUTIVES LOOK FOR HOME STINT

MUMBAI: 'It is better at home' seems to be the mantra of a number of Indian nationals working overseas. Uncertainties triggered by the pandemic, family proximity and competitive compensation packages are some of the reasons for Indian nationals to return to the country and look for job placements.

According to data collated by Russell Reynolds Associates on leadership candidates placed by the firm in India in the last four years, in 2021, 17% of the Indian nationals returned from a job abroad. This data point is the highest in four years, with the average from the previous three years being 12%. (More...)[12]

---

[12] *Full story at:*
https://timesofindia.indiatimes.com/business/india-business/overseas-desi-execs-look-for-home-stint/articleshow/90341678.cms

CHAPTER XX

EPILOGUE

Allow me to end with a disclaimer or three.

This book was originally written sometimes in 2003-2005. No attempt was made to publish it at that time because, first, I did not think this, as a book, had a market. Second, finding a publisher willing to take a risk on a book of this nature would have been well neigh impossible. Marketing this book, finding readers for it in sufficient numbers to make the investment worthwhile, would have been even more difficult. Self-publishing, publishing as an e-book directly, or using the popular platforms available nowadays, was simply beyond one's imagination at the time when the book was originally written, hence was not an option. This book is seeing the light of day today only because such platforms are easy to come by nowadays.

As is evident, this book was written from my experience that is at least two decades old. In the meanwhile, much water has flown down the Danube, the Amazon and the Nile. Times have changed, so have the people, their attitudes, the economies and what's described in this book. Therefore, take the 'facts', comments and suggestions in this book with a generous pinch of salt, if you will. Update your information before venturing out. This author or its publisher will not be responsible for any consequences arising out of any action taken by anyone based on the contents of this book.

In order to retain the original flavour, I have not attempted to update the contents at most of the places in this book. Therefore, E&OE. Take this book as a blast from the past. Enjoy it simply for whatever these pages have to offer.

Stay healthy, stay safe. Keep smiling.
Asante Sana.
RB